Open Secret

Also by Wei Wu Wei

Open Secret

WEI WU WEI

SENTIENT PUBLICATIONS, LLC

First Sentient Publications edition, 2004

Reprinted in the United States by Sentient Publications, by arrangement with Hong Kong University Press, Hong Kong.

Chapter 6, "I Am Not, but the Universe Is My Self," chapter 53, "Seeing It Simply," and chapter 54, "The Essential Identity," are reprinted by kind permission of the Editor of *The Mountain Path* (issues of January, July, and October 1964), Shri Ramanashramam, Tiruvannamalai, S. India.

Grateful acknowledgment is made for permission to use Matt Errey's editorial notes.

Cover design by Kim Johansen, Black Dog Design
Book design by Anna Bergstrom

Library of Congress Cataloging-in-Publication Data

Wei, Wu Wei.
  Open secret / Wei Wu Wei.-- 1st ed.
    p. cm.
  ISBN 1-59181-014-0
  1. Buddhism--Doctrines. 2. Suffering--Religious aspects--Buddhism.
I. Title.
BQ4235 .W45 2003
294.3'42--dc22

                                    2003018029

Printed in the United States of America

10 9 8 7 6 5 4 3 2

SENTIENT PUBLICATIONS

A Limited Liability Company
1113 Spruce St.
Boulder, CO 80302
www.sentientpublications.com

Inscription

"A single word is sufficient to reveal the truth."
—*Shên Hui*

In case such a word be lurking somewhere herein . . .

To Each Reader

This work is essentially a discussion; if occasionally passages should appear to be didactically expressed, please be so good as to interpret them as emphasis, due to a rift in the cloud of misunderstanding which we are mutually seeking to disperse. The writer of these lines has nothing whatever to teach anyone; his words are just his contribution to our common discussion of what must inevitably be for us the most important subject which could be discussed by sentient beings.

W.W.W.

Contents

Part V

Preface

As LONG as subject is centred in a phenomenal object, and thinks and speaks therefrom, subject is identified with that object and is bound.

As long as such condition obtains, the identified subject can never be free—for freedom is liberation from that identification.

Abandonment of a phenomenal centre constitutes the only "practice," and such abandonment is not an act volitionally performed by the identified subject, but a non-action *(wu wei)* leaving the noumenal centre in control of phenomenal activity, and free from fictitious interference by an imaginary "self."

Are *you* still thinking, looking, living, as from an imaginary phenomenal centre? As long as you do that you can never recognise your freedom.

Could any statement be more classic?
Could any statement be more obvious?
Could any statement be more vital?

Yet—East and West—how many observe it?
So
Could any statement be more needed?

Note: Wu Wei merely implies absence of volitional interference. Whom do I mean by "you"? I mean "I." I am always I, whoever says it, man or monkey, noumenally or phenomenally, identified or free—and there is no such entity.

P.S. If you have understood the above it is quite unnecessary for you to read any more of this book.

Part One

❦

Bye and bye comes the Great Awakening, and we find that this life is really a great dream. . . .

Then we are embraced in obliterating Unity. There is perfect adaptation to whatever may happen—and so we complete our allotted span.

Chuang Tzu, ch. 11

1 ·— *Time and Space*

WE TEND to misunderstand the nature, and exaggerate the importance, of "time" and "space."

There are no such "things" (they do not exist in their own right): these come into apparent existence, i.e. they "function" only as a mechanism whereby events, extended spatially and sequentially, may become cognisable. They accompany events and render their development realisable. In themselves they have no existence whatever. They are appearances, and their apparent existence is deduced from the events they accompany and render perceptible. They are hypothetical, like the "ether," symbols, like algebra, psychic inferences to aid in the cognisance of the universe we objectify, and they neither pre-exist, nor survive apart from, the events they accompany, but are utilised in function of each such event as it occurs.

Where there is no event there is no need of "time" or of "space"—and in their absence we are no longer in bondage—for there is no one to believe that he is bound.

Time is only an inference, devised in an effort to explain growth, development, extension and change, which constitute a further direction of measurement beyond the three that we know and at right-angles to volume; and "past," "present" and "future" are inferences derived from this temporal interpretation of the further dimension in which extension appears to occur. All forms of temporality, therefore, are conceptual and imagined.

Thus prophecy or precognition is perception from a further direction of measurement, beyond that of time, a fourth right-angle, wherefrom—as in the case of each superior dimension—the inferior ones are perceived as a whole, so that the "effects" of "causes" are as evident in what we call the future as they are in what we call the past.

The event only occurs in the mind of the perceiver of it, singular or plural as the case may be, and no event could be anything but a memory when we know it. No event is anything but a psychic experience. Events, or memories of events, are objectivisations in consciousness.

2 ⌁ *The Pseudo-Problem of "Suffering"*

WHO IS there to suffer?

Only an object could suffer.

I am not an object (no object could be I), and there is no I-object nor I-subject, both of which would then be objects.

Therefore I cannot suffer.

But there appears to be suffering, and its opposite, both pleasure and pain. They are appearances, but they are experienced. By whom, by what, are they experienced?

They are apparently experienced, and by means of an identification of what I am with what I am not, or, if you prefer, by what we are not, illusorily identified with what we are.

What we are does not know pain or pleasure, what we are does not, as such, know anything, for in neither case is there an objective entity to suffer experience.

Whatever intensity sensations may appear to have, in the dream of manifestation they are effects of causes in a time-sequence, and apart from the time-sequence in which they develop they *are not* either as cause or as effect.

There is no one to suffer. We appear to suffer as a result of our illusory identification with a phenomenal object.

Let us at least understand.

What we are is invulnerable and cannot be bound.

3 · ~ The Will-Inference

I

THE MECHANISM of living seems to be based on the notion that what sentient beings do is due to an act of volition on the part of each such phenomenal object.

It is obvious, however, that they react rather than act, and that their living is conditioned by instinct, habit, fashion, and propaganda. Their way of life is primarily a series of reflexes, which leaves a limited scope for deliberate and considered action; that is, purposeful action which, superficially considered, might appear to be the result of volition, or what is called an act of will.

Nevertheless "volition" is only an inference, for, search as we may, we can find no entity to exercise it. All we can find is an impulse which appears to be an expression of the notion of "I." It would seem to be unjustifiable to assume that such an impulse could be capable of affecting the inexorable chain of causation or, alternatively, the process of manifestation which produces apparent events, unless itself it were an element of one or of the other.

II. *Volition*

Volition, then, would seem to be an illusory inference, a mere demonstration on the part of an energised I-concept, resulting either in frustration or fulfillment and thereby being the source and explanation of the notion of *karma*. Sentient beings are entirely "lived" as such, as has often been noted by philosophers and endorsed by metaphysicians, and the psycho-somatic phenomenon is inexorably subject to causation. That is why sentient beings as such, as the Buddha is

4

credited with stating and re-stating in the Diamond Sutra, *are* not as entities. That, also, is why, since as phenomena they are *not*, noumenally—though they cannot *be* as entities or as anything objective—nevertheless, they *are* as noumenon.

And noumenon, by definition being integrally devoid of any trace-element of objectivity, is *not*, cannot *be*, in any sense whatever—since all forms of being must necessarily be objective. Here language fails us and must be left behind like the raft that has carried us across the river. All we can say is something such as "this, which is all that sentient beings are, itself is not."

If this is not understood it will appear unsatisfying but, if understood, it will appear luminous and revelatory, and for the obvious reason that the understanding is "itself" this noumenon which we are.

But here the eternal reminder is necessary: phenomena which, as the term asserts, we *appear* to be, are nothing but noumenon, and noumenon, which is all that we are, though as such itself is not, *is* as phenomena (as its appearance).

"Volition," therefore, though it is not—is only an appearance phenomenally—*is* noumenally and may be regarded as an objectivisation of noumenality. As such we know it as *buddhi* or *prajna*, as intuitional inseeing and, knowing it, it is ourselves, all that we are, which—in the knowing of it—we are knowing, for this which we are *is* this knowing of it.

All very simple, evidently, until you try to objectify it in words.

III. Definition of Volition

Perhaps the question of volition may be most readily understood just by asking who there is to exercise volition and who there is to experience the results of it.

Phenomenally there is an apparent cause, which can be called ego-volition, and a psychic effect, which may be fulfillment or which may be frustration.

The effect of conditioned "volition" is the result of causes of which the volition is a mediate effect-cause, and an apparent psycho-somatic apparatus experiences that effect.

And as regards that "volition" which is non-volition, *wu wei* or *bodhi*, the ultimate effect is integration.

In order that there might be volition and the result of volition there would need to be an entity to exercise the one and to suffer the other. If it is found that there are no such entities then no such thing as volition can exist other than as a concept.

Noumenally there is no volition—because there is no I. Phenomenally spontaneity alone is non-volitional.

But by understanding what volition is not, the way may be found to be open whereby that "volition" which is non-volition may liberate us, as apparent objects, from the bondage which is due to that identification with an objectivisation, which we have never been, are not, and never could be.

IV. Observations

Living non-volitionally is a contradiction in terms (unless it implies being "lived").

Not reacting to events as a result of understanding this is living non-volitionally (or being "lived").

Intellectual understanding is a conditioned cause. Intuitional understanding might be a non-mediate cause.

For cause and effect are divided in Time, but Intemporally they are one.

4 ·~ Saying It Simply

I

ONLY AN object can suffer, but phenomenally subject and object, being one whole, spin like a coin so that the intervals between *pile et face* (heads and tails) are imperceptible. Consequently pain, or pleasure, appear to be continual.

Noumenally, on the contrary, there is no object to suffer pain or pleasure. Noumenon is invulnerable, and cannot be otherwise. Noumenon is the unmanifested aspect of what we, sentient beings, are: Phenomenon is our manifestation.

Therefore, manifested, we must suffer pain and pleasure; unmanifested, we cannot experience either. Both aspects are permanent and coeval, the one subject to time (which accompanies all manifestation, rendering the extension of events perceptible), the other—timeless.

Noumenon—timeless, spaceless, imperceptible being—is what we are: phenomena—temporal, finite, sensorially perceptible—are what we appear to be as separate objects. Phenomena, subject to time, are impermanent, illusory figments of consciousness, but they are *nothing but* noumenon in manifestation, in a dream context (one of several dream contexts—psychic conditions due to sleep, drugs, asphyxiation, etc.). Similarly noumenon is nothing; factually, demonstrably, cognisably (and therefore objectively) is nothing, that is, no *thing, but*—apart from—its manifestation as phenomena.

That is the meaning of the "mysterious" contradictions enunciated by the Sages: "Form is nothing but void, void is nothing but form," "Samsara is Nirvana, Nirvana is Samsara," "Phenomena and Noumena are one," etc., etc.

That is why Huang Po can say:

"People neglect the reality of the 'illusory' world." (*Wang Ling Record,* p. 106)

"On no account make a distinction between the Absolute and the sentient world." (p. 130)

"Whatever Mind is, so also are phenomena—both are equally real and partake equally of the Dharma-Nature. He who receives an intuition of this truth has become a Buddha and attained to the Dharma." (p. 111)

"All the visible universe IS the Buddha." (p. 107)

But quoting Hui Nêng he can also say, and often in the same context:

"There's never been a single thing,

Then where's defiling dust to cling?"

"Full understanding of this must come before they can enter the way." (p. 111)

"Finally, remember that from the first to last not even the smallest grain of anything perceptible (graspable, attainable, tangible) has ever existed or ever will exist." (p. 127)

And lastly:

"On seeing one thing , you see ALL." (That is, all perceiving is Buddha-mind, the living-dream is itself Buddha-mind.) (p. 108)

"Hold fast to one principle and all the others are identical." (p. 108)

What, then, is this principle?

"Once more, ALL phenomena are basically without existence, though you cannot now say that they are non-existent. . . . Moreover, Mind is not Mind. . . . Form, too, is not really form. So if I now state that there are no phenomena and no Original Mind, you will begin to understand something of the intuitive Dharma silently conveyed to Mind with Mind. Since phenomena and no-phenomena are one, there is neither phenomena nor no-phenomena, and the only possible transmission is to Mind with Mind." (p. 106)

"Moreover, in thus contemplating the totality of phenomena, you are contemplating the totality of Mind. All these phenomena are intrinsically void and yet this Mind with which they are identical is no mere nothingness." (p. 108)

This, chapter 37 of the Wan Ling Record, is probably the clearest and most valuable statement of the ultimate truth that we possess. In this he states, as quoted, that in seeing one thing you see ALL. What is this one thing, and have we seen it? It surely is just that phenomenon and noumenon are one. In differentiating between Appearance and its source, neither of which exists other than conceptually, we must never forget this "one thing"—which is that they are one.

However, if we see this one thing as "one," we have not seen it, we have missed it. It is not "one thing," for a thing is an object. In fact we can never "see" it, for here, this is the seeing which is non-seeing, in which no "one" is seeing and no "thing" is seen as such.

Have we not understood? Can we not perceive intuitively what this must be? An eye cannot see itself. That which is sought is the seeker, the looked-for is the looker, who is not an object. "One" is a concept, objective therefore, and "it" is *devoid of any trace of objectivity." (Huang Po, p. 35)

We cannot see (find, grasp, attain, touch) it, because "we" are not at all objects, nor is "it" an object, and whatever "we" are noumenally is what "it" is noumenally. Thus we are one—and there is no such object as "one" in noumenon, since, as we have just read, there is no such thing (object) as noumenon either.

This is the non-seeing, by non-seeing which you see ALL, the one principle with which all others are identical, the one problem which, solved, solves all others at once, the centre of centres from which all can be perceived.

II

But phenomenal objects, noumenon in manifestation, although they are nothing but noumenon, and can know that, even realise it via their phenomenal psychic mechanism called "intelligence" etc., cannot "live" it in their individual, space-time, conceptual existence, which is subject to the temporal and illusory process of causation. Although it is all that they are—and despite the fact that in it, therefore, they have nothing to attain, grasp or possess—in order that they may "live" it in any sense apart from having objective understanding of what it is, that is, of what they are, they must de-phenomenalise themselves, disobjectify themselves, disidentify their subjectivity from its projected phenomenal selfhood, which is dominated by a concept of "I."

This adjustment has been given many names but is nevertheless not an event or an experience—for, except as an appearance, there is no object to which such can occur; it is a *metanoesis* whereby a figmentary attachment or identification is found not to exist, nor ever to have existed—since it is a figment. This displacement of subjectivity is from apparent object to ultimate subject in which it inheres, from phenomenon to noumenon, from illusory periphery to illusory centre (for infinity can have no centre), from supposed individual to universal Absolute.

This is awakening from the phenomenal dream of "living," confined within the limits of sensorial perception and suppositional "volition," into the impersonal infinitude of noumenality in which every possible problem of phenomenal "life" is found to have vanished without leaving a trace.

Ed. Note: All Huang Po quotations above taken from "The Zen Teaching of Huang Po: On the Transmission of Mind" by John Blofeld. Grove Press, New York. 1st pub. 1958)

5 ⤳ *Geometrically Regarded*

FROM EACH further dimension all antecedent dimensions can be perceived as a whole; for example, cubic space or volume contains within itself length and breadth (i.e., plane surface) and height. Does it not follow that we must necessarily be seeing volume from a further, a fourth, direction of measurement, and consequently, that in order to perceive that, we would need to observe from a fifth?

So we observe the universe of phenomena, which appears to us in three directions of measurement—length, width and height—from a fourth direction, which might be what we know as duration but whose geometrical character we may only be able to perceive when we develop the ability to observe from a further direction at right-angles to those with which we are already familiar.

Phenomenal seeing, then, is normally in three dimensions observed from a fourth. That is the perceiving of appearance as volume. It is likely, however, that some sentient beings only perceive in two dimensions—length and breadth, or plane surfaces, horizontally or vertically—and that the third, volume, is an inference of which they are not conscious, although it is from that that they are looking.

If phenomenality may be equated with tri-dimensional perception, then may we not assume that the essential characteristic of noumenality is perception from a further direction? Should that be so, then—geometrically regarded—what we term "Awakening" is waking up to a further field of vision, that what we term "Liberation" is freedom from the limitation of the cubic vision within which we have been confined, and "Enlightenment" is the sudden brightness of a further "universe" encompassing the three in the limited darkness of which we have been groping; i.e., that these are three terms for the displacement of the subject to a centre from which he can perceive objects in a further, richer, and more complete perspective.

If this should be so, then those who are "awakened," perceiving a further dimension—*that one from which we normally observe and which therefore is ours*—are themselves perceiving from a still further direction, from a fifth. If, then, there were any entity to perceive the "awakened," such entity would perceive the fifth dimension from a centre in the sixth.

Here metaphysics may intervene in order to point out the illusory futility of the purely theoretical notion of a perpetual regression. There could be no entity, there is only a perceiv-*ing* anyhow, and the whole process is phenomenal interpretation of noumenality. This, then, is within the illusory science of phenomenality, and may only enable us to understand the *apparent* mechanism whereby a phenomenal object can come to know noumenality.

We know—from the words of the Masters, unless from our own experience—that "Awakening" is accompanied by the immediate, if not simultaneous, abolition of all phenomenal "problems." It is like knocking out the bottom of a barrel, by which all the confused, and so "impure," contents of our phenomenal mind (phenomenal aspect or reflection of Mind) vanish. Instead of solving problems one by one, like striking off the heads of a Hydra, which grow again, all disappear simultaneously and forever (as an effect), like stabbing the Hydra herself in the heart.

But is not this the exact counterpart of what we have sought to establish geometrically? We have suggested that a displacement of the centre of the supposed entity (pseudo-centre) to a further, more profound centre will reveal a further dimension wherefrom all inferior dimensions are perceived in a greater perspective. Assuming that this is the ultimate perspective, or even if it is not, even if there be perspectives *ad infinitum*, is this not precisely a description of the mechanism of what the term "Awakening" connotes?

6 ～ *"I Am Not, but the Universe Is My Self"*
—SHIH T'OU, A.D. 700-790

Logical Analysis of This Intuition

OBJECTS ARE only known as the result of reactions of the senses of sentient beings to a variety of stimuli.

These stimuli appear to derive from sources external to the reagent apparatus, but there is no evidence of this apart from the reagent apparatus itself.

Objects, therefore, are only a surmise, for they have no demonstrable existence apart from the subject that cognises them.

Since the subject itself is not sensorially cognisable as an object, subject also is only a surmise.

Since the factual existence of neither subject nor object can be demonstrated, existence is no more than a conceptual assumption, which, metaphysically, is inacceptable.

There is, therefore, no valid evidence for the existence of a world external to the consciousness of sentient beings, which external world is therefore seen to be nothing but the cognisers of it, that is—sentient beings themselves.

But there can be no factual evidence for the existence of sentient beings, either as subject or as object, who therefore are merely a conceptual assumption on the part of the consciousness in which they are cognised.

It follows that "consciousness" also can only be a conceptual assumption without demonstrable existence.

What, then, can this assumption of consciousness denote? This question can only be answered in metaphysical terms, according to which consciousness may be regarded as the manifested aspect of the unmanifested, which is the nearest it seems possible to go towards expressing in a concept that which by definition is inconceivable.

Why should this be so? It must be so, because conceptuality cannot have conceptuality for source, but only the non-conceptual, because that which objectively conceives must necessarily spring from the objectively non-existent, the manifested from non-manifestation, for conceptuality cannot conceive or objectify itself—just as an eye cannot see itself as an object.

Therefore consciousness can be described as pure non-conceptuality, which is "pure" because unstained either by the conceptual or the non-conceptual, which implies that there is a total absence of both positive and negative conceptuality.

Not existing as an object, even conceptual, there can be no "it," there is no "thing" to bear a name, no subject is possible where no object is, and total absence of being is inevitably implied.

All we can do about this which we are, which to us must be objectified as "it" in order that we may speak of it at all, is to regard "it" as the noumenon of phenomena, but, since neither of these exists objectively, phenomenally regarded it may be understood as the ultimate absence from which all presence comes to appear.

But consciousness, or "Mind," does not "project"—the phenomenal universe: "it" IS the phenomenal universe which is manifested as its self.

Metaphysics, relying on intuition or direct perception, says no more than this, and points out that no word, be it the Absolute, the Logos, God, or Tao, can be other than a concept which as such has no factual validity whatsoever.

This-Which-Is, then, which cannot be subject or object, which cannot be named or thought, and the realisation of which is the ultimate awakening, can only be indicated in such a phrase as that quoted above:

I am not, but the apparent universe is my self.

7 ⌁ *Gone with the Mind*

THE PAST is gone. But the Present has become the Past before we can know it, i.e. before the complicated phenomenal processes of sense-perception, transmission and conception have been completed. Therefore the Present has gone too.

And the Future? We cannot know it until it has become the Past—for it can never be known in the Present. Then how can it be at all, for we cannot know the Past (which is gone)? Surely we cannot: neither Future, Present nor Past can we ever know.

How, then, do they exist—if existence they have? And if any of them exist, which exists? Or do all of them exist as a unity unextended in time and space, a time and space which only come into apparent existence with them, hypothetically, in order to render them cognisable?

Clearly none of them exists as a thing-in-itself, as objective events in their own right, as phenomena separate from the cognisers of them.

Future—Present—Past appear to be three illusory aspects of a single subjective phenomenon known as "cognition."

8 ⋅- *The Fasting of the Mind*

PHENOMENAL LIFE in an apparent universe is nothing but objectivisation: all that we know as "life" is only that process.

Living, for the ordinary man, is a continual process of objectifying. From morning till night, and from night till morning, he never ceases to objectify except in dreamless sleep. That is what manifestation is, and it is nothing but that, for when objectifying ceases the objective universe is no more—as in deep sleep.

But when Ch'an monks "sit" they seek to empty their minds, to practise a fasting of the mind, for while the mind "fasts" there is no more conceptualisation; then no concept arises, not even an I-concept, and in the absence of an I-concept the mind is "pure" (free of objects); then, and only then, it is itself, what-it-is and as-it-is. When that is permanent it is objectively called enlightenment, when it is temporary it can be called *samadhi*.

In that state of fasting the mind is only "blank" in so far as there is a total absence of objects; itself it is not absent but totally present, then and only then. Nor is "objectivising" replaced by "subjectivising"; both counterparts are absent, and the subject-object process (whereby subject, objectifying itself as object, thereby becomes object, which object is nothing but subject), the "spinning of the mind," ceases to operate and dies down. The mind ceases to "do"; instead, it "is."

In the absence of objectivisation the apparent universe *is not*, but we *are;* which is so because what we are is what the apparent universe is, and what the apparent universe is—is what we are; dual in presence, non-dual in absence, sundered only in manifestation.

9 ·— *Aren't We All? . . .*

I

HAVE YOU noticed? How many of us, writing our thoughts about Buddhism, even the purest Ch'an, express our thoughts in such a way that a sentient being is envisaged as a medium, that is, by inference, having objective existence? Is this still not so even when the very subject of our thesis is the non-existence of a self? Indeed, how many of us are there who do *not* do this? Let us even ask how many texts are there in which this is not done or implied?

Yet many of us seem to know that it is not so, that it cannot be so. Surely we have read the Diamond Sutra, perhaps many times, in which the Buddha is credited with having said again and again in varying contexts that there is no such thing as a "self," a separate "individual," a "being," or a "life"? If we have not seen for ourselves that this must be so, would it not be reasonable to expect that we would provisionally take it on trust from the lips of the Buddha, and apply it?

Alas, no. It is too hard, too much to ask: conditioning is too powerful. Yet without that understanding, that *basic* understanding, that *sine qua non*, for what can we hope? However much else we may have understood, have we in fact even started on the way—the pathless way that leads no body from no there to no here? We have no phenomenal masters, no *gurus*; our masters, our *gurus* are immanent. What a sad, sardonic smile they seem to wear when we look within!

II. Who Done It?

"What did you say?" "Who are they?," "Who is writing all this?" Well, who is reading it? Who is there to do, or to appear to do, the one or the other? Really, really, what a question! Who indeed! Why, no one, of course; who could there be? Surely that is evident, axiomatic, elementary? From the beginning there has never been a single "who," as Hui Nêng approximately said; "who," utterly absent noumenally, is ubiquitous phenomenally.

Whoever asks the question, that is "who?"

He is the seeker who is the sought, the sought who is the seeker.

He done it!

10 ᴗ *Utter Absence as Us*

DESPITE APPEARANCES to the contrary, nothing that is other than conceptual is done by a sentient being, for a sentient being objectively is only a phantom, a dream-figure, nor is anything done via a psycho-somatic apparatus, as such, other than the production of illusory images and interpretations, for that also has only an apparent, imagined or dreamed, existence. All phenomenal "existence" is hypothetical. All the characteristics of sentient beings—form, perceiving, conceiving, willing, knowing (the *skandha* or aggregates)—are figments of mind which "itself," i.e. as such, also is hypothetical only.

Each and every action, every movement of each, in the extension and duration imagined so that they may be sensorially perceptible (that is, in the framework of space and time) are dreamed or imagined by a dreamer which has no quality of selfhood, of objective being—that is to say, by hypothetical mind.

This hypothetical mind is the Perceiving, Discriminating Division of mind in its subjective aspect phenomenally conceived, and the Perceived, Discriminated Division in its objective aspect, but the perceived is the perceiver, the discriminated the discriminator, and the subjective and objective aspects only appear as dual in manifestation. We are the former: we appear to be the latter, but they are not two unmanifested.

All that is cognisable is part of the phantasy of living, all that we can think of as ourselves is an integral part of this hypothetical universe; sentient beings are totally therein and in no way or degree apart from it, as they often suppose when they imagine themselves as instruments whereby the objective universe is produced, for it is produced not by, but with them as one of its manifestations.

This is more readily perceived in the case of a dream, which we can consider when awake, whereas in the living dream we are still asleep; i.e., "ourselves" are the dreamed figures, phenomenal objects of the dreaming subject in the dream of living.

Our dreamed "selves," autonomous in appearance, as in life, can be seen in awakened retrospect to be puppets totally devoid of volitional possibilities of their own. Nor is the dream in any degree dependent on them except as elements therein. They, who seem to think that they are living and acting autonomously, are being dreamed in their totality, they are being activated as completely and absolutely as puppets are activated by their puppeteer. Such is our apparent life, on this apparent earth, in this apparent universe.

All this which is dreamed is the product of the dreaming mind, of the subject-object process called "causation," within the consciousness in which it occurs; it is integral in consciousness, it is consciousness itself, and there is nothing else whatever that IS. But "consciousness" is only a concept *as such*: it is no thing, no object, has no subject therefore. It can only be indicated as the Unmanifested, and even such indication can only be a manifestation of the unmanifested.

But these elements in the dream, in either dream, are not nothing in the sense of annihilation. Viewed "noumenally" they are "something" indeed. They are whatever their dreamer is, whatever This-Which-Dreams them is, indeed everything in the dream is the dreamer thereof, and that, as we have seen, is the subjective aspect of consciousness—for object *is* subject, the subject which in-forms it, which is subsistent to it. Therefore this "something" which they are is "everything": objectively, phenomenally everything, which, subjectively, noumenally, is "nothing," but which as "nothing" is still everything, total absence phenomenally, which is total presence noumenally. Everything is nothing, nothing is everything, for neither either is or is not, and only is-ness is by neither being nor not-being.

It is *as the subjective aspect of consciousness* (not as the objectivised aspect) which is all that they can be said to BE, that sentient beings dream the universe by objectivising it.

11 ⁓ Echoes – I

THE IDEA of a separate individual, an ego, self or I-concept, is an object. I become an object—inevitably—every time I think of my self. Also, every time I act as my self it is an object which acts.

Once in a while, however, I act directly—but then no "I" acts.

"I" am not conscious of anything: never. "Consciousness" as such is all that I am.

The Positive Expression

Noumenon is the sub-stance of phenomena, whose being it is, the being of Noumenon being the being of Being as such—which is the absence of Non-being.

Void is the sub-stance of Form,

Form is the manifestation of Void.

Again

There is no cogniser apart from the "thing" cognised; there is no "thing" cognised apart from the cogniser of it. But the "cogniser" is only an act of cognition (a cognising), of which the "thing" cognised is the counterpart.

Therefore the "cogniser" and the "cognised" are not different, "not two": they can only be the "function of cognising," the functional aspect of pure potentiality, which, as such, has no phenomenal or objective existence apart from its manifestation as cogniser-and-cognised.

The observer cannot observe the observer.

The Asker is the Answer.

"If you suppose that anything is NOT Prajna, let me hear what it is."—*Hui Hai*, p. 118.

So why call it "Wisdom"?

Definition of "Noumenal Living"

To be in non-objective relation with all things is to live noumenally.

To live without volition is to be in non-objective relation with all things.

Ceasing to objectify, or pure thought antecedent to "name and form" (interpretation) is living without volition.

That is the *nien* of *wu-nien*, the *hsin* of *wu-hsin*, the *wei* of *wu-wei*, "moved only by the Will of God." *(Chuang Tzu)*

୨୧

You have no objective existence (as "you"),

Nor any subjective existence (as "you"),

Because "existence as subject" would make subject an object—which it could never be.

You only exist as existence itself.

Hara-Kiri

If attachment must be renounced, renunciation itself must also be renounced.

But renunciation, being also an act of volition, it is volition that must renounce itself.

Can we renounce what we have never possessed?

What is there to "do" or to "have" anything?

Let us start by locating this "we."

Inseeing

Everything is what we are: every object is its subject, and what we *are* is "our" subject.

Noumenal seeing is enlightened seeing, phenomenal seeing is unenlightened seeing: that is the only difference between them.

How so? Because noumenal seeing sees phenomena noumenally—and then phenomenon is as noumenal as Noumenon itself.

ॐ

Identified with non-being, you can only be a mirror. "One must become identified with non-being and mirror the whole, for the truth is one and final."—*Hsieh Ling-yün* (A.D. 385-453)

12 ⸱- *The Cosmic Continuum*

A CIRCLE HAS only one centre. But the cosmic circle, being infinite, has an infinite number of centres, and each one is the centre of the whole, which, on account of its infinitude, is neither a circle nor not a circle, so that its centre, also, is neither a centre nor not a centre.

Therefore the centre, being ubiquitous, is itself the circle, and the notion of individual centres within the infinite circle is a vain and superfluous concept.

Metaphysically such is a diagram of the cosmos, and a simple illustration of the position of phenomenal beings in a five-dimensional phenomenal universe, in which they are neither something nor nothing, neither centres nor not centres—for they are at the same time the centre and the whole.

13 · Past, Present, and Future

THE PAST is a mnemonic impression of an event extended in duration, the extension being a psychic device to render the event perceptible and conceivable as a consecutive incident. There is no such "ens" or "thing-in-itself" as the "Past," which only implies an "event" that has been extended in imagination into a succeeding "event" and so on *ad infinitum*.

The "past," therefore, is only a method of indicating re-placed elements in the seriality of extension in a hypothetical "time." The "past" has no autonomous existence whatever, nor has the "present," which is purely theoretical, since it has no duration, and the "future," which is only a speculation concerning the possible extension of events in the same hypothetical seriality.

The serial development of any kind of dream-story is an aspect of the mechanism of its presentation, whereby it is elaborated conceptually.

The attribution of actuality to such contrivances, however ingenious, is gratuitous.

"Life," therefore, as a series of events, is imagined and not "lived," as every kind of dream is, and "Time," if anything at all, is surely and very literally "all my eye"!

Note: "Causation," dependent on "Time" (duration, extension) is a laboratory instrument only, and itself, as a "thing" entirely illusory.

14 · Who Is There to Be Enlightened?

I DON'T BELIEVE that there is anyone to wake up! Sentient beings are not *there* at all as such—as the Buddha pointed out in the Diamond Sutra, so how can they wake up? And *what* is there to wake up? They are concepts or thought-forms, objects—and objects cannot either go to sleep or awaken! What nonsense all that doctrine must be! It all begs the question, for phenomenally they are appearances, and noumenally they are not asleep.

The subjective element of mind is awake, and always has been, untouched by any concept such as that of time. But the dreamer seems to become identified in split-mind with his own dreamed object. So the identified personal dreamer always has to wake up: it is always the individualised dreamer which awakes—not his dreamed objects. There can be no awakening for dreamed objects in any kind or degree of dreaming.

Dreamer, Awake!

Living is dreaming too. The "dreamer" becomes identified with his object and snores loudly. "He" and his objects dream and dream, in which every act of the objects is in-formed by the dreamer. In the degree of such in-forming by the dreamer the dreamed objects "exist." But they are totally dreamed, totally in-formed; therefore they partake totally of the "existence" of the in-forming dreamer.

In fact, however, the appearance that is dreamed is nothing but the source thereof which is dreaming. But it is only the in-forming source which can awaken: the objects as such have never slept, and cannot awaken; of themselves they have never been at all, for they cannot have any nature of their own. Nor has the in-forming mind of either dream any nature of its own, for mind, whole or split, is *non-entity*.

Note: Objects are purely imagined in *all kinds of dreams*. They are ropes seen as snakes, in the old analogy, when even the ropes were never there non-phenomenally. That is all we are as objects.

15 ·- *Tathata*

"SUBJECTIVITY," NOT having any objective existence, can never die—for therein is no thing to suffer extinction, nor can "it" be born—for therein is no thing to come into being. Therefore "it" must be eternal (*aeternitus*, that is beyond the concept of "time").

Only objects can be born and can die, only objects can be perceived, only objects can be thought of or conceived, only objects can appear to exist. And all that "exists" is appearance (phenomena) only.

About what is indicated by the word "subjectivity" nothing whatever can be cognised, not because "it" is *some thing* that is not cognisable, but because by definition "it" is not any "thing" at all. And yet, and inevitably, "it" must necessarily be all that is and all that we are.

What, then, is it? No sort of "what." Just sheer phenomenal absence, whose *absence* is us (THIS which we are).

16 ·- *Seeing*

I

HOW CAN there be a "seeing"? Surely the "seeing" is false; the object is not over there, it is at home "here." I am it, it is I. How, then, can I "see" it? There is no object there: therefore there cannot be any subject here.

All my eye! My eye and whatever lies behind it.

II. Once More

The conclusion is simple and evident. There is no one to "see" and no "thing" to be "seen"; the "seen" is the "see-er" and the "see-er" is the "seen," and that is a definition of noumenon. This applies to each of the senses by means of which phenomena are cognised.

"Noumenon" has no more existence than "phenomena" since each is merely a concept of divided "mind," itself the sixth sense, interpreter of its fellows. And all that each *is* is neither "there" nor "here" nor any "where."

No name, nor any description, can ever be given to what remains, for that is by definition no object, because as ultimate subjectivity it could not see itself which is therefore no "thing" other than objectified as every "thing," i.e., all phenomena.

Therefore "it" is ultimate and absolute phenomenal absence and the absence of that concept of "absence," which is *absolute presence*.

Note: Phenomena are noumenon objectifying itself, or Noumenon is subject objectifying itself as phenomena.

17 ·- The Logic beyond Logic

As LONG as one is employing concepts, as long as our mind is split, every such concept is subject to the Double Negative (*Shen Hui*, A.D. 686-760) or the Theory of Double Truth (*Chi Tsang*, A.D. 549-623), that is to say that noumenally it neither is nor is not, but the moment whole-mind is invoked there is no longer a question of dual counterparts, of a perpetual regression; for instance "total phenomenal absence is total noumenal presence" (total disappearance of being is total appearance of non-being) no longer need imply some "thing" beyond dual concepts.

It no longer need imply noumenally that *neither* either is or is not, but states that both, thus, absolutely are. Phenomena are Noumenon, Noumenon is phenomena, being becomes empty and emptiness becomes being—as the early sages expressed it—so that what is dual is not dual, and what is not dual is dual.

Expressed otherwise, once the statement is understood split-mind is no longer objectivising by means of dual concepts: the process of objectivising is transcended, functioning has returned to the source and whole-mind is functioning directly.

Total noumenal presence and total phenomenal absence are ONE as they stand: never can they be two, there is no beyond; whatever a logician may maintain semantically, this statement is final and states the absolute in so far as that can be stated.

Semantically there appear to remain five concepts— "noumenal and phenomenal," "presence and absence" and "one." That is so—as long as there is an entity, or supposed entity, objectifying these concepts, i.e., occupied in conceiving objects. As such they are not—"it is the mind, not the flag or the wind, that causes the apparent movement."* But there is no such entity, the supposed entity has vanished: impersonal "mind"—whole-mind which objectively is not—the source, which is not objectively, which, therefore, is neither "noumenal nor phenomenal," "present or absent," nor "one" (which also is an objective concept), which is pure and total non-objectivity, alone is in question.

---

* *Ed Note:* Hui Nêng

Philosophically this is indicated by saying that all that we are is the absence of our phenomenal absence, i.e., the absence of an *I-entity*, an "ens," to conceive our phenomenal absence.

Note: The moment the subsistent notion of any entity is abolished, whole-mind alone remains, the pseudo-centre which unceasingly objectivises is automatically abandoned, and mind may be said to reintegrate its source.

Phenomena may be said to be Noumenon objectifying itself, or Noumenon may be regarded as Subject objectifying itself as phenomena, neither phenomena nor Noumenon having any objective *existence*.

18 ·– Is the Man-in-the-Moon in the Puddle?

WHAT CAN be the utility of exposing this or that object, or all objects, as "empty" or "void," *en détail ou en bloc?* It is not the *objects* as such that are this or that, "real" or "empty," for they are not anything we can call them, except the mind which is perceiving them, and that "mind," being only a name, is just the perceiving itself.

Objects are *neither k'ung* (empty) *nor* not-*k'ung:* they are just their subject, their source.

Judging objects is as futile as all "problems" are, for only *the mind itself* is concerned. All judgements and "problems" vanish when split-mind is made whole. Judgements and "problems" are like cutting off the heads of a Hydra, which grow again; let us turn to the source and tackle the Hydra! The revelation of Hui Nêng in the monks' dispute as to whether the flag or the wind was moving, settles that perfectly for all time.

Object-subject (absence of both as separate concepts, before they are split) are not then dual; i.e., subject becomes object, and object becomes subject, or being becomes "empty," and "emptiness" becomes being, duality is non-dual and non-duality is dual. In short, if you return objects to their source, that source is the responsible cause of their appearance, but their *appearance* is nevertheless inseparable from its source, so that trying to affect (act upon) objects as such is as absurd as trying to cure diseases via their symptoms, to affect substance via its shadow, or objects themselves via their reflections.

If your phenomenal objects are returned to whole-mind, instead of being judged by split-mind, there will be nothing to judge—for they too are whatever that whole-mind itself is.

19 ∙– Suggestions

NEED THERE be purpose—since there is no choice?

❦

All I am is "see*ing*" when I see,
All I am is "hear*ing*" when I hear,
All I am is "sentience" when I feel,
All I am is "understand*ing*" when I know.

❦

True-seeing is non-seeing—no one looking.
True hearing is non-hearing—no one listening.
True action is non-action—no one doing.
True thinking is non-thinking—no one thinking.
Spontaneity alone is non-volitional—and there is no I.

"That which hearing is—is beyond thought, mind and body."
(Surangama Sutra) What is heard is the hearer thereof.

The totality of an action is in function of the totality of the absence of the performer thereof. That alone is pure action.

Unborn and Undead

There is neither birth nor death; birth and death are objective only.

Objective living is *phenomenal*. This which we are is not phenomenal: a shadow is not its substance. But it has no existence apart from its substance.

Comedy

Phenomenal objects apparently desperately hunting for themselves as subject! How could an object seek its subject? All it *is* is subject, and all it does is done by subject, so that subject itself is desperately hunting for itself!

Comment

The "subject" which they then find that they are is no entity, for *subject can never be that.*

Once more: the subject of object is itself an object as "subject," just as the object of "subject" is itself nothing but subject. That is, they are one, and how they are one, two sides of a single coin, without the coin: they are subject and object alternatively and at once.

Is this semantic jugglery? Perhaps, but it could never be

anything else, for it can be understood but cannot be expressed as a logical proposition. It might help, but would change nothing, if the words "object" and "subject" were replaced by the words "phenomena" and "noumenon." All phenomena are nothing but noumenon, and there is no such thing as noumenon: *noumenon is "noumenon" only as phenomena*. Thought of, they appear as two things, but they *are* not even as dual concepts: as such they are both phenomenal. They are one whole—and that is no thing.

This understanding is, perhaps, the essential understanding—and it cannot be syllogistically expressed.

❧

Even the best writing is like taking pot-shots at the moon.

20 ·⁓ The Mechanism of Appearance (As It May Be Conceived)

THE APPARENT universe neither arises *via*, nor independently of, sentient beings. The apparent aspect of sentient beings arises *with* that of the universe, and the universe becomes apparent concurrently.

Their sentience is responsible for their interpretation of arisal, or manifestation, their sentience being the *perceptive* aspect of "mind," and their appearance being the *perceived* aspect, as is that of all phenomena.

The apparent difference between what are known as animate and inanimate objects is inexistent objectively, that is as objective phenomena, but, subjectively, non-apparent sentience, though as such it does not occasion arisal or manifestation (which is causal), is responsible for perception.

One might say that sentient beings as phenomena arise, are manifested, "directly," like all phenomena whatsoever, but that the apparent universe *as known to sentient beings* is an indirect arisal, or manifestation via their sentience, such sentience being expressed by means of cognitive faculties (known as the *skandha*), themselves conceptual, but *in itself* a direct manifestation of whole-mind.

Can this be made clearer by saying that sentience is that aspect of arisal, or manifestation, by means of which phenomena are cognised as such, although itself is not responsible for their arisal? Sentience may be seen as an expression of the dynamic aspect of manifestation (whereas appearance itself is the static aspect), by means of which the faculties of cognition interpret, but are not causative elements in, such manifestation.

The mechanism here described is all purely conceptual: this is not, therefore, a description of anything factually existing, but a schema illustrating the position and function of apparent sentient beings in the phenomenal universe in which objectively they are integral, but in the perception, conception and interpretation of which they constitute a functional element.

Metaphysically nothing of this kind can be said to *be*, for the mechanism of causation is entirely phenomenal.

Metaphysically there is only the apparent manifestation of non-manifestation, of which latter nothing whatever can be cognised since it has no objective quality whatever, and sentient beings themselves are nothing but what "it" IS.

21 ·- *Hommage à Hui Nêng*

Replacement of Responsibility

THE USUAL displacement of responsibility is on to the object! But objects have none whatever: total responsibility lies with their subject.

Bring it home! Keep it at home!

Where is the flag flapping, and *what* causes it to flap?

Where is the cow-bell ringing, and *what* causes it to ring?

Where is the shoe pinching, and *what* causes it to pinch?

Where is the odour of the rose, and *what* causes it to smell so sweet?

Where is the flavour of the wine, and *what* gives it that flavour?

Where is the knowledge of these phenomena, and *what* causes them to be known?

Re-establish responsibility where it belongs. Return it to its source (which it has never left).

Return every thing to its source, to which it belongs, and which it has never left!

That is the practice of non-practice.

22 ·- *To Hell with It All!*

FOR GOODNESS' sake let's give up all this objectivising nonsense! It has gone on altogether too long! Wasting our apparent lives objectivising from morning to night, and from night to morning—except for deep sleep when we go sane for a short respite.

Take the absurd idea people have about there being a moon in the sky! What is a "moon," what is a "sky," and where is either the one or the other to be "inside" or "outside" the other or the one? Did you ever hear such balderdash?

We know perfectly well, you who are reading this know perfectly well, where the so-called "moon" comes from, where it belongs, and the so-called "sky" along with it! They belong with all the other phenomenal objects we objectify day and night, dreaming "asleep" or dreaming "awake"—rhinos and roses, beetles and bodhisattvas, dandelions and dragons.

Aren't you heartily sick of them all? No? Very well, then, admire them, do what you like with them, but for Heaven's sake don't go on thinking that they "exist" as such in some sort of way somewhere or other "over there," "up there," "down there" or any other sort of "where"!

You know quite well where they "exist," how they "exist," and that their only "existence" is at home where they belong, which is where you perceive them.

That is living practice.

23 ⤳ *Echoes - II*

HOW CAN A shadow eliminate itself?

⟡

There are no "things" (objects) apart from the cognising of them: there is no cognising apart from the "thing" cognised, *because there is no cogniser.*

That is the naked truth, and it is why phenomena and noumenon are not two, nor Samsara and Nirvana, object and subject, etc., etc. *ad infinitum*—and full understanding proceeds therefrom.

❦

There is no such "thing" to aim at, seek or look for, as what one is. On ceasing to seek or to look—one is present.

❦

"Being" is "becoming," since it comports duration. Every sentient being—being nothing but mind itself, can find mind itself, mind his, her, or our self, just by ceasing to search, for the act of searching is precisely that which, by externalising itself turns itself away from this which it is.

❦

This which is free is not an entity,
That which is bound is not what you are,
This which is unconditioned is void,
That which is conditioned is not you.

❦

Any apparent advance in which your self is of the party is only going round in a circle.
Why? Are you anything but a rumour?

❦

Of every direct perception, however luminous it may be, we should know that to the majority of the readers of its expression it will appear nonsensical, to a minority a mystery, and to a very few a faint reflection of a luminosity that glimmers within themselves.

For it is the nature of such expression to appear impenetrable to the deductions of the objectivising mind.

All things considered,
Bondage is wholly the notion of "I,"
And liberation is liberation from the idea of liberation.
Is there any one to be bound, any one to be free?
So what?

An "I" of which one is conscious is an object.

Whatever you may be, you are being "lived." You are not travelling, as you think: you are being "travelled."

Remember: you are in a train. Stop trying to carry your baggage yourself! It will come along with you anyhow.

"Pure Thought" is seeing things as they appear—without arguing (thinking) about them, just "seeing, seeing, seeing," as Rumi said. Above all, without *inference*.

All Said and Done

Everything is I, and I am no thing.

All phenomena are subjective manifestations (objectivisation of subjectivity). What I am objectively is the totality of

37

phenomenal manifestation. What I am subjectively is all that all phenomena *are*.

Nothing personal about it anywhere or at any stage. The personal notion is not inherent and is the *whole trouble*.

Part Two

⚭

What do you have to do?

Pack your bags,
Go to the station without them,
Catch the train,
And leave your self behind.

Quite so: the only practice—and once.

24 ∙- *The Logic of Non-Logic*

The Meaning of "Noumenon"

The phenomenal is conceptual—appearance or form, the interdependent counterpart of which is *the non-phenomenal,* which is also conceptual—non-appearance or formlessness.

The source of the phenomenal and the non-phenomenal ("the world of form and the formless world" as the Masters referred to them) is *noumenon.*

"Noumenon," therefore, is not the interdependent counterpart (or the opposite) of "phenomenon" but the source of "phenomena and of non-phenomena." All this is purely conceptual.

Phenomena are both positive and negative, both appearance and non-appearance, form and non-form, both presence and absence of form or of appearance, for each is dependent on the other and can have no hypothetical existence apart from the hypothetical existence of the other.

"Noumenon" is a symbol indicating double phenomenal absence—the absence of both counterparts or, as sometimes expressed, the absence of the negative counterpart (a double absence), which is also the absence of the absence of the positive.

Even as such, philosophically speaking, "noumenon" still appears to be dualistic; that is, to be an objective concept requiring a "cogniser" of some "thing cognised." But here there is *no thing cognisable,* and precisely because "it" (noumenon) is also the cogniser, and indeed all hypothetical cognisers that ever were or ever could be.

As such "it" is unfindable, unknowable, simply because "it" *could not be* as an object of anything but "itself" and "it" could never know "itself" as an object, so that the symbol is just a phenomenal ruse contrived in order to indicate some "thing" which is not such. Referring to "it" as "Suchness" or "Tao," or in any other way whatever, is equally futile logically—since "it" is the supposed cognising element, the supposedly cognised, and the apparent act of cognition.

25 ⁓ *Living Without Tears*

THERE CANNOT be any such thing as "non-volitional living"; taken as a verb it is in fact a contradiction in terms, for the act of living non-volitionally must constitute an act of volition—the volition of non-volition. Like other negatives it is a mode of its positive, as its positive is a mode of itself.

But the fact, not the act, indicates something which phenomenally can be, for it can imply "being lived," whereby "non-volitionally" is understood, since there is no place for volition in the process of *being* lived.

Since, however, there is every reason, total evidence, to suppose that we are in fact lived, entirely and absolutely lived, like all dreamed figures in every sort and degree of dream, there cannot be any such factor as volition in the serial development of our lives.

"Volition," then, is not an effective element at all in phenomenal life, but one that is imagined to be such. It is in fact an expression of an I-concept, an "ego" appearing to function, and as such may be seen as pure clowning, a psychic activity which, by pretended interference in the chain of cause-and-effect, produces the reactions recognised as satisfaction or frustration, according to whether the attempted interference has been in accordance with what had to occur or has been opposed to that.

Volitionally inhibiting "volition," therefore, in no way

factually effects the serial evolution of our lives, in no way has any impact on events, and endeavouring to abolish "egotic" volition can only reinforce it by such an exercise of itself. For instance, when we are told to "lay everything down," that means abandoning volitional activity—for everything we are required to "lay down" is a supposed effect of supposed volition, and it could only be "done" by a voluntary act, that is by a supposed "ego" or independent "self"; from which it follows that such is nothing more than an act of clowning or mummery.

If, then, it can effectually be done it must be a result, an effect of cause, and that cause can only be in the chain of causation which cannot in any degree be affected by an act of will on the part of a supposed "ego" or I-concept. Such cause can only arise as an effect of prior causes which, in such a case as that under consideration, can only appear as a result of understanding, the development of which may be described, somewhat metaphorically, as "our" only freedom. (It is, of course, not "ours," and phenomena cannot have "freedom," which anyhow is only a concept applicable conceptually to them, but perhaps the "noumenality" which in-forms phenomena manifests directly so that understanding may arise or "appear.")

Therefore non-volitional living, "laying down" everything by an abandonment of volitional activity, or "letting ourselves be lived," can only be effected by non-action (*wu-wei*); i.e. as a result of understanding arrived at by identification with the noumenality of *prajna*; that is, as an *effect* of *in-seeing*.

No apparent volitional interference is involved, nor, if it were, could it have any bearing on the effect except in so far as its absence or latency, the non-arising of ego-activity, leaves the mind open for the direct or intuitional apprehension which is represented by the picturesque Sanscrit concept called "prajna."

The intuition, indeed, is direct, but the result appears to us as indirect, for, to us, what we regard as "direct" is a supposed effect of "volition." That is integral in the illusion of separate individuality and the notion of an "ego" or I-concept, just as "volition" is the apparent expression or activity of that, whereas in fact non-volitional life or being-lived is direct living, spontaneous living, *wu wei*, and at the same time is living without tears.

26 ·— Why We Cannot Be

ALL EXISTENCE is objective.

We only *exist* as one another's objects, and as such only in the consciousness that cognises us, for our experience of one another is only an act of cognition in mind and in no way asserts the experiential existence of the object cognised.

Our objective existence, therefore, is in mind only; that is, it is merely conceptual.

As regards subjective existence—is not that a contradiction in terms? That implies an objectivisation of subject, which as subject-object represents the hypothetical "being" which we imagine that we are. Subjectively there can be no "us."

Thereby is clearly demonstrated our total "inexistence" other than as concepts in consciousness.

27 ·— Transcendence and Immanence

I AM THE dreamer of myself in the dream in which I appear, but *as such what I am is not the objective (dreamed) appearance,* and so I am no entity.

It is not the object that awakens, but it is the identification of the dreamer with his object that causes the illusion of bondage.

Awakening is disappearing, dissolving, vanishing as an object. Awakening is the *dissolution of appearance*, the evaporation of a dream or an illusion.

Awakening is the dis-appearance of phenomenality (of the objective, of all objectivity as such). Awakening is the discovery that the apparently objective is in fact "subjective," and the apparent entity has dis-appeared with the total appearance.

28 ·- Integral Seeing

SEEING PHENOMENA as noumenon is true seeing.

It is seeing noumenally—that is, in non-objective relation with "things," instead of seeing phenomenally—which is in objective relation with "things."

Seeing phenomenally is seeing phenomena as *our* objects.

Seeing noumenally is seeing phenomena as our selves, as all they are, as their source and as our source. It is very precisely not seeing them as our objects but as their subject, not objectively but subjectively, not as being "without" but as being "within." It is reuniting the separated with their *integer* which is all that we are.

Such true seeing, therefore, is no-seeing (of some thing by some thing), ultimately neither seeing nor non-seeing—since there is then no object to see or not to see, and no subject of no object.

It is re-absorption, re-union, re-identification of the dis-united, making split-mind whole, at-one-ment.

Note: True seeing might perhaps be indicated by the term "apperceiving" as sometimes used herein.

29 ∙- *Rumours - I*

In Both Kinds of Dream

WE ARE all part of the party: the party goes on even if we fall asleep, but our falling asleep is also part of the party.

Do you remember?
When you look at a reflection of the moon in a puddle you are the moon looking at itself.

You are merely an inference. Only *objects* are knowable.
So they must be all you can know of yourself.
Therefore the apparent universe is all that you are as a "you."

We are required to cease looking at objects as events apart from ourselves, and to know them at their source—which is our perceiving of them.

Your only self is other—there is no other that is not yourself.

Until we know what we are not,
Which is the inferential phenomenon
That we think we are,
We can never know the immensity
Which is our noumenal non-being.

Intention can make you a saint,
But it can prevent you from becoming a sage?
Appearance only: there is no entity to be either.

All forms of practice are learning to kill dragons.

"You look like a man riding a tethered horse."—*Chuang Tzu*, chapter XIII, p. 138
Each of us spends his time "riding a tethered horse."
The horse cannot be set free;
But each of us can forbear to ride.

How can it or anything be an illusion? What is the "it" or "anything"? There is no "it" or "anything" to be illusory! Since there is nothing to be illusory—there is no such thing as illusion.

Nor, then, is there any thing to be *anything*, even to be not—to be or not to be.

That is true seeing.

❧

Owing to misuse of words one should not say, "Don't meditate!" One has to say, "Don't call it 'meditation' if it is not, but if it is—don't do it!"

❧

It is not for me or another to accept your notion which you call "meditation": it is for you to give whatever you do a name which suggests what it is and not what it is not! Only then will it become possible to discuss it.

Words *must* be used in a sense which is in accordance with their etymology or, at *least*, in a sense accepted by a dictionary.

❧

Unless you hate you cannot possibly love.
And vice-versa.

30 ⟿ "Alive, Alive-O"

SURELY TO-DAY, and increasingly, there is an exaggerated tendency to overestimate the importance of the fact of living—of our apparent existence as individual phenomena? It is almost a dictum to say that we "have only one life," and "must make the most of it"—understood.

Whatever the origin of this, it seems to be great nonsense, and thoroughly demoralising. In the first place is there any evidence, let alone likelihood, that it is a fact? Is it not more probable that "we" have far too many? That, certainly, is the view of the oriental majority of the human race.

And even if that were definitely not so, what is this "living" of a "life," subject to conceptual "time," and who or what "lives" it? The notion of the "sacredness of life"—human only *of course!*—is somewhat unevenly distributed over the surface of the Earth.

Dreams and poppycock! Let us find out what in fact we are—and then the importance and apparent duration of this phenomenal experience will seem to matter very little indeed!

"A long life, and a merry one!" By all means, and why not? But does it matter? Do we bother about the longevity of— say—fish?

Note: "Life" is only manifestation expressed in a space-time context, entirely hypothetical; there is in fact no "thing" whatever to begin or to end, to be "born" or to "die," and our experience is a psychic phenomenon.

31 · They Said It Was Simple

STRANGE TO say—and how rare it is!—the term "phenomena" implies precisely what etymologically it says. Every thing, every conceivable thing, which our senses, and our mind (which interprets what our senses perceive) cognise, is exactly an "appearance," i.e., an appearance in consciousness interpreted as an event extended in space and in duration and objectified in a world external to that which cognises it. And simultaneously that which cognises it assumes that it is the subject of the cognition and, as such, an entity apart from that which is cognised.

As long as these associated assumptions subsist, the correlated assumption of "bondage," and the painful sensations accompanying that assumption, must necessarily remain intact.

Therefore release from this assumed "bondage" can only be obtained by comprehending the falsity of these assumptions which are responsible for the presumed bondage, for both "assumptions" and "bondage" are apparent only, i.e. are purely phenomenal.

"Appearance" is precisely what the word implies, i.e., something that "seems to be," not "something that is."

If this is realised—and how obvious it should be, since the terms themselves say it precisely!—the psychological elements of a purely psychological bondage are severed, and only the psychological conditioning occasioned by that "bondage" remains, and this, like all conditioning, will dissolve as a result of a process of de-conditioning which consists in the establishment of the concept of "appearance" (phenomenon) in place of the concept of "reality."

The dissolution of that which is cognised as "real" and "separate," as events extended in space and time, necessarily involves the dissolution of the assumed cognising entity, and both are then seen as phenomena, or appearance, in consciousness.

When this readjustment is effected both subject and object no longer exist as such, and no entity remains which could be conceived as being "bound." That is—bondage is no more.

How very simple indeed it is!

Note: "Then who am I?" If anyone could tell you that, what you were told would necessarily be nonsense—for it would be just another object, as phenomenal as the rest. Some day you will know automatically what you are—which is what the Masters meant when they said so often, "You will know of yourself whether water is tepid or cold"—or, you will just be that knowledge.

32 ᛫᛫ The Disappearance of Subject

THE REASON why ignorance and knowledge are identical is because all objects are objectivisations; enlightenment and ignorance are also identical, for both are objective concepts.

He who has lost his objective self thereby loses his subjective self, and has found his non-objectivity—which is the absence of subject and object.

Objects are neither "empty" nor "non-empty," not because they are not this or that, but because of themselves they are no "thing" whatever, *but their source only*.

The reason for comprehending the emptiness of objects is the abolition thereby of their subject, an abolition which remains impossible as long as the objects are perceived as real; since the one is the counterpart of the other, they have no independent identity. Phenomenally, therefore, they are one concept that has a dual aspect, and noumenon is its source.

Since subject can never be abolished directly via itself, the recognition of its objects as appearance only results in the dis-appearance of itself as a supposed object functioning as their subject.

33 ᛫᛫ Let's Talk It Over!

THE QUALITY of "emptiness" or of "non-emptiness" of an object has no direct bearing on the efficacy of the procedure implied by the use of those terms, for it is only the *inexistence* of the object itself *as such* that is being indicated: the object can neither be "empty" nor "non-empty" nor anything else, for it is not *there* to be anything or to have any quality. To state that the object is empty, void, or whatever word may be chosen, is begging the question—for then the object is still there to be that, to have that quality or the lack of that quality.

This understanding is a step towards the further understanding that the apparent object is to be located at its source, and not in its manifested appearance.

The Indian analogy of the clay and the pot, and the Chinese analogy of the gold and the lion-image, created by the potter and the goldsmith from the clay and the gold respectively, are imperfect also and really rather misleading, for they too carry on the old and futile attempt to represent by objective images and concepts THIS whose total character is non-character, whose sole being is non-being, whose only objective existence lies in the absolute absence of objectivity and of non-objectivity.

The sole aim of the statement, as of the analogies, is to throw the mind back, to turn it away from objectifying, and return it to its true centre, which is precisely the ultimate non-objectivity from which objectivity springs.

Concurrently this destruction of the concept of the object as a thing-in-itself, or as an objective reality, operates psychologically to the same end in that, by annihilating the object as such, the subject of that object—the immediate subject which reveals it conceptually—is automatically annihilated also. This is inevitable because phenomenal subject and phenomenal object are inseparable, two aspects of a single functioning, and can never be apart at any moment or in any circumstances.

So that when this understanding is applied to all objects, to all phenomena whatever, subject is thereby always eliminated, and it is the elimination of the subjective illusion that matters rather than that of its objective counterpart. The subjective illusion, based on separate individuality, an ego or will-body, operating by supposed volition, can never be annihilated *directly*—for that would be by means of itself. This, the negative way, is the only possible means of eliminating the pseudo-subject of pseudo-objects, which is the sole factor obstructing our knowledge of this which alone we are, which prevents our "being" it—though we are it, which prevents our "living" it throughout our phenomenal manifestation.

There is every reason to suppose and to believe that the moment this understanding becomes spontaneous (that is, the moment we are able directly and unconsciously, entirely non-volitionally, to perceive in this manner—which is direct perception antecedent to name-and-form, prior to temporal interpretation by the objectivisation-process of "spinning" subject-object) we shall be free of our apparent bondage—for our apparent bondage is just that. This spontaneous direct perception is precisely what the Masters meant when they spoke of the One True Thought, the Thought of the Absolute, or, in the words of the great Shên Hui (668-760), the successor of Hui Nêng: "*Silent identification with non-being* is the same as that which is described as sudden enlightenment. So also what is described as 'when a single thought is in accord (with the truth) at once you have the ultimate wisdom of the Buddha.'" ("Wisdom," here as elsewhere, i.e. *Prajna*, means "Subjectivity" or Non-objective understanding, as Han Shan told us). This is the "single thought" in question, and that is the reason why the elimination of the objective reality of objects is stressed as the essential method of understanding.

Note: Referring to the enlightenment of the Abbot Ming by Hui Nêng the Sixth Patriarch, Fung Yu-lan says: "The force of the Patriarch's question was to eliminate subject and object. When a man as a subject and its object are eliminated then he is one with 'non-being,' and is described as having silent identification with non-being; and by that is meant that not merely the man knows there is non-being but that he is actually identified with non-being." (*The Spirit of Chinese Philosophy*, trans. E.R. Hughes, Kegan Paul 1947, p. 166. Also his *History of Chinese Philosophy*, trans. Derk Bodde, Princeton University Press 1952, Vol. II, p. 397. The former, a slight volume, is perhaps more readily accessible.)

34 ⸱⁓ Non-objective Relation

Self-portrait

A NON-OBJECTIVE RELATION to oneself is not to think of oneself as an object—not any kind of object, physical or psychic.

To know that oneself has no objective quality whatever, has absolutely nothing objective about it, is devoid of any trace-element of objectivity, is surely to know what one is, which, in metaphysical terms, is just the absence itself, the very absence, *of the absence,* the total lack of any objective character, nature, or quality, that is the absence of the idea of the absence as of the presence of the perceptible and the conceivable.

Portrait of You

A non-objective relation to others, to all phenomena sentient or non-sentient, is ceasing to regard them as the objects of oneself.

Knowing that *as objects* they can only be appearance in consciousness—that is, without nature or quality in themselves (as phenomena)—this understanding is merely the elimination of misunderstanding, of what is technically called "ignorance."

We know also that our objective (apparent) selves are equally devoid of nature and quality, so that both supposed subject and its supposed objects are instantly seen to be appearance only.

We then realise that what we all are is not different, and that is at-one-ment.

There is no "love" in it—for love is an expression of separateness—and that crude form of affectivity called "emotion" is replaced by pure affectivity, which is probably what is meant by *karuna*, and which is closely associated with what may be indicated by the word "joy." We do not then "love" others: we "are" others and our phenomenal relation with "them" is simple, direct, spontaneous.

It is immediacy and its sole nature is joy.

35 ·~ "Where, Oh Where? . . ."

I

WHY IS what-I-am neither without nor within? Because I am measuring from "my" own head.

That is the ubiquitous and perpetual error.

"My" own head is not the centre from which any but phenomenal distance can be measured, and the centre of what-I-am is not there.

Where is it? It does not lie in any "there": it is in every "here," and any "here" lies in every "there."

"My" phenomenal head is not outside what-I-am, for what-I-am has no "without"; nor is "my" phenomenal head inside what-I-am, for what-I-am has no "within."

The centre of what-I-am, phenomenally, lies in every "where" and, noumenally, lies in no "where"—for every and no "where" are identical.

When I perceive directly, "my" head is only an elaborate conceptual interpretation on the part of divided mind objectifying as subject-and-object, and then that concept returns to its source and takes "my head" with it.

When, upstream of conceptual interpretation, I thus perceive directly, the inferential subject of that inferential object must be absent also.

Having no objective "head," there can be no "me" left not to have that eliminated object.

At that moment I am—but there is no moment, no where for that moment not-to-occur, and no "I" to be.

Note: These few lines seek to carry further than his simple expression of it, a thought of Maharshi's in his last poem. I do not know whether that is what he wished us to do?

II

Is it enough just to ask Who? Is it not necessary also to ask Where? and When?

We tend to think that with the disposal of Who? there will remain a solid objective universe, complete in all respects apart from the apparent defection of our precious selves.

But things are not in fact like that at all! It is desirable to realise that the *Lebensraum* of each precious self shares the fate of its subject, whatever that fate may be, for whatever is sensorially perceived and cognised with his objective appearance is integral phenomenally with that. Also the duration which was imagined in order that each element or event might evolve in perception, will no longer come into apparent existence in the absence of such elements or events and of their medium.

It follows that wherever there is an objective Who? to be found there will be an objective Where?, and an objective When? also, but in the absence of the one the others will be absent also.

But, since the phenomenal Who? does not disappear as an appearance, nor does the phenomenal universe, as a consequence of the apperception that all phenomena are appearance only, the identification with an object is destroyed, and the consequent liberation is not only from Who? but also from Where? and from When? The supposed phenomenal "subject" has ceased to believe in the impossible, and knows at last what he has always been, and what the phenomenal universe always has been—which knows no Who?, no Where?, no When?

But the spectacle goes on, and the phenomenal "subject," also, however wide awake he may be. For him Who? Where? and When? are meaningless terms, though he continues to use them as others do, such "others" being as meaningless, in their sense of "meaning," as Who they may "be," Where they may "be," or When they may "be," and his only motivation is an urge to bring them to the same understanding of the fictitious character of what they suppose to be genuine and of the genuine character of what they suppose to be fictitious.

36 ·- *Quod Erat Demonstrandum*

Nobody believes that he does not exist,
Nobody ever has believed, or ever will believe that he does
    not exist.
Why is that?
Because there is no entity to believe that he does not exist.*
    That is what is meant by saying that he neither exists
    nor does not exist.**
What, then, is he?
He is the absence of that which he is not,
Which is all that he can think that he is.

37 ·- *I-I: This Universe Which We Are*

When subject looks—subject sees object.
When subject is seen looking at object
Subject becomes object, and is no longer subject.
    When subject looks at itself, it no longer sees anything, for
there cannot be anything to see, since subject, not being an
object as subject, cannot be seen.

---

* If there were an entity to believe that he did not exist he would
thereby exist.
** There is a solution of continuity between what he is and the concept "existing/non-existing," i.e., like that between the moon itself
and the concept of its reflection in a puddle.

That is the "mirror-void"—the absence of anything seen, of anything seeable, which subject is.

But it is neither "mirror" nor "void" nor any thing at all.

It is not even "it."

That is the transcendence of subject and object—which is pure is-ness.

That is what is—the total absence which is the presence of all that seems to be.

Perhaps it could be said better, but there can be little more to be said.

Note: I-I was Sri Ramana Maharshi's term for an ultimate Self.

The "mirror-void" is a resplendent shining mirror which reflects the phenomenal universe, revealing every thing and retaining no thing.

38 ·- As Long As . . .

As long as we believe that that-which-we-are is objective,

As long as we think that there could be something objective in us,

As long as we do not find laughable the idea that there could be anything whatever objective in what we are,

As long as we say the word "I" with the idea that I could be any kind of entity,

As long as it is not invulnerable-I, I-untouchable, I-unnameable, I-inconceivable which is acting directly,

We are bound.

Because bondage is only identification with a phenomenal object, and because identification is precisely this idea that this-which-we-are is an object, psychic or somatic.

Released from this conditioned idea of our personal

objective existence,
We are FREE.

Note: It is not enough to think of that-which-we-are-not: it is necessary *not to think* of that which-we-are not. It is necessary that all that we could possibly be shall act directly. Direct action, like direct perception, is anterior to discriminating thought and knows not "volition."

39 ·— Practice? By Whom, on What?

"ILLUMINATION" IS pure subjectivity, phenomenally a subjective state: how could the manifestation of an appearance affect its source?

Phenomena cannot act upon noumenon—for an act is phenomenal. A shadow cannot act on its substance—for an appearance cannot affect the source of its appearance.

All apparent action, and so all practice, necessarily has its origin in noumenon. Who, then, practises?

It is noumenon alone that "practises," and phenomena are "practised." To what end?

But practiser and practised are one, objectively separated as what they are not, as appearance, but noumenally united as what they are.

There is no practiser, and there is nothing to practise.

40 ·~ *Speaking of God . . .*

I

WHAT IS God?

    What a question! How could there be such a thing?

    The belief is widespread.

    No doubt, but God could not be an object.

    What then?

    God is Subject—ultimate subject of all objects.

    Including ourselves?

    Subject of the subject-object which we think of as ourself.

    Then, as subject we are objects?

    Conceptually, yes. "We" act as subject and think of ourselves as objects incessantly, spinning like a coin, alternatively "heads" and "tails," but in all we are or could be subjectively we are whatever Godhead is.

    And what is that?

    Just the absence of what we suppose ourselves to be, which is the presence of what we *are*.

    And that is?

    Our total objective absence, which is necessarily the subjective presence of God.

Note: This does not imply the disappearance of objective phenomena as such: it is concerned with the disappearance of *identification* with an objective phenomenon assumed to be what we are. We are not *that:* we are *this*—and *this* is no "thing"; therefore we are no "thing."

II

    You say that God is not an object! Why not?

As an object, God is one of a hundred objective gods. Can you not see that it must be so?

The idea is unfamiliar. The latter are idols.

If God is conceptualised, God is just a god. Every concept of God is an idol. *Every prayer or offering to an object*, material or conceptual, *is prayer or offering to an idol*.

That is offensive, blasphemous!

Offence and blasphemy lie in the mind in which the idea of them arises. I am merely drawing attention to the obvious.

Can one not blaspheme intentionally?

It is impossible to blaspheme an object, an idol; it is only possible to cause the notion of offence to arise in the minds of the worshippers of that object, or idol.

Although God, as such, is rarely portrayed, members of some Christian Churches understand that an image of a deity or saint, although an object of prayer and offering, is not for them an idol. It is just a symbol. What are you smiling at?

Shakespeare has a word about the sweetness of the perfume of roses however named. We are not concerned here with the sincerity of beliefs, however innocent, but with metaphysical insight.

What, then, *is* blasphemy?

Any and every action performed otherwise than in the presence of God. You will find it implicit in the Gospels, and stated in the *Bhagavad Gita*.

The presence of God suggests to me the presence of an object, an idol!

Alas, I feared it might be so! By the presence of God is meant the absence of the presence of self—or just the immanent divine nature.

41 ·– Rumours – II

The practice of meditation is represented by the three famous monkeys, who cover their eyes, ears and mouths so as to avoid the phenomenal world. *The practice of nonmeditation* is ceasing to be the see-er, hearer or speaker while eyes, ears and mouths are fulfilling their function in daily life.

You

If time is the fourth dimension of space, the temporal projection of Subject results in an inferential *entity* as *object*.

∝

In order to answer any question about what one is—mind would have to be divided into subject and object, and then the answer could not be the true or whole answer.

∝

When insight evaporates in words,
Only resonance survives.

∝

The Masters appeared to attack the reality of objects, but it was the seeing of objects that they were pointing at.

Such was the case also as regards objective images (objects in mind): negating them, they sought to arouse a flash of understanding of their conceptual nature, and recognition of the source of all ideation.

Noumenally there is no entity to be bound,
Phenomenally there is no entity to be free.

There is nothing theoretical about Ch'an: it is immediate,
not mediate, understanding.

What I am is whatever God is.
The supposed mystery, so incomprehensible, is only due to
seeking the truth as an object.

There is no humility, but only degrees of pride.

"I have no mental processes that would be of use, and no
Way to follow."—*Hui Hai,* p. 103

Not exercising the apparent function of will is Tao.

Practice

Many Buddhists seem to be trying to awaken the dreamed

figures instead of the dreamer of them. When the dreamer awakens the dreamed figures disappear, for their manifestation is over. That is why there are no "others," but only dreamed figures.

It is the dreamer of each dream that must awaken, the dreamer of the identified dream, whose dream-figures disappear. He is the identified dreamer, not the impersonal dreamer of the total cosmos.

The enlightened state is the state of non-being and of non-identity.

The identified man takes part: the unidentified looks on!

Part Three

❧

The Heart Sutra

The burden of the Heart Sutra
Is not the nature of objects
But the seeing of them,
Which is what they are.

42 ·~ Concerning the "Heart Sutra"

Section I

The *Hrdaya*—usually called the Heart Sutra—is commonly said to represent the quintessence of the Prajnaparamita doctrine. Its importance is so well understood that it is recited daily in monasteries, a practice which does not necessarily lead to its general understanding.

This rendering is based on the three principal sources— Sanscrit, Chinese and Tibetan, but it is not a direct translation. The rendering of some technical terms is given in Notes, but the meaning of words in general has been checked with the Sanscrit or Chinese. It pretends to nothing beyond a possible clarification of the essential burden of the Sutra, whose meaning is obscured by objective and, so, inapposite terminology.

The accepted title itself is questionable, and should be questioned. In the East the heart was regarded as the seat of what we think of as the mind, whereas to us the heart is a symbol of the seat of feeling. Therefore the translation of *hrdaya* or *hsin* as "heart" is clearly misleading. This has been generally realised, so that modern translators usually render these words as "mind." But translators are loath to abandon their scholastic conventions, even when they know them to be inadequate. Could they sometimes be placing their own reputations as scholars above their duty to reveal the truth— in so far as that may be done?

The case of the title of this Sutra is slightly different because the word "heart" to us is also a symbol of a living centre, and the term "prajnaparamita" has been given the meaning of "perfection of wisdom," so that the phrase "the heart of the perfection of wisdom" makes a very pretty title which will not readily be abandoned.

I have already dealt with the word "heart" (*hrdaya, hsin*), and will now make a few observations concerning "prajna-paramita." In colloquial and general literature the word "prajna" in all forms and combinations is concerned with knowledge and understanding, and can be rendered as "wisdom," and "paramita" implies "crossing over" and, exceptionally, "complete attainment" or "perfection." Therefore, as we should have expected, the translation "perfection of wisdom" is impeccable scholastically. But these words were used in a highly technical sense in Buddhism, in a sense that varied according to the context and the epoch, and even the locality, and these senses—which we may call jargon if we wish—rarely, if ever, bore the colloquial and general meaning.*

The Chinese had the great good sense to leave these terms untranslated, phoneticising them as *pan-jo* and *pa-rami*, whereas we are such pedants that we have to try to translate them without having any word that could convey their meaning. *Paramita* can be summarily dealt with because it bears the meaning of "transcendent," and that will be found to be adequate in the majority of contexts, but "wisdom" or "sagesse," apart from being too general, does not even *suggest* the technical meaning of *prajna*.

In the first place *prajna*, as the functional aspect of *dhyana*, cannot be abstract, nor can it be passive, nor any objective

---

* A Chinese scholar remarked to me recently, "Buddhism in China is another language." Buddhism having a language of its own, the use of colloquial terms in translation cannot transmit the thought of the original.

"thing," such as "wisdom": it may be indicated as an active principle, the functioning of *dhyana*, as *dhyana* is the static aspect of *prajna*. From this, in passing, it may be observed that *dhyana*, in its technical sense, has nothing whatever to do with "meditation" except that, in the etymological meaning of that word, it might signify almost anything but that.

In the second place we are plainly told what *prajna* means, although that could not be necessary to anyone who understood the scriptures and the teaching of the T'ang dynasty masters. Han Shan, a fully enlightened Sage, in his commentary on the Diamond Sutra, informs us that by "prajna" the Buddha wished us to understand "subjectivity." That does not mean that every time the word "prajna" appears it can just be rendered as "subjectivity"; it merely implies that wherever and however the term may be used it invariably should have a subjective implication. In other words: it can never, when properly used, indicate any thing objective or anything that can be objectivised, either physically or conceptually. As has been stated, the term occurs in many different shades of meaning, which no existing term in English or French could hope to cover, and, the objective nature of language being what it is, occasionally it will be found rather loosely, if not improperly, employed in a dualistic context in order to indicate a function of mind or an attribute that is frankly objective. The masters were not often philologically-minded: they were concerned with manoeuvering the minds of their monks, and with pointing in a direction different from that to which the monks, like ourselves, were conditioned. And occasionally they pointed towards some understanding—by apparently stating the opposite.

I do not know the degree of authenticity of the available Sanscrit texts, of which there are said to be about twenty in existence. The Tibetan text, however, appears to have considerable differences, though not in essentials. The Chinese text used is that translated by the great and famous monk Hsüan Tsang (A.D. 596-664) who brought it himself from India with so many other Sutras, though in fact he is known to have been acquainted with the Sutra before he left China, for he "used" it *en route*. I do not know to what extent it may have suffered from the errors of copyists. It has elements which are different again from the other versions consulted. There were five Chinese translations, the third made by Kumarajiva, the fifth being the one by Hsüan Tsang.

The *Hrdaya* could perhaps be regarded less as a *résumé* of the immense Prajnaparamita Sutra than as an original and dynamic reaction to all scriptures, to all the doctrines, methods, practices, dogmas, in fact all the ecclesiasticism of religious Buddhism. In a few dozen words, within a conventional setting, all the basic Buddhist teachings are summarily dismissed, not iconoclastically but as gently as could be, by quietly enumerating the subjective elements of individual personality, then their objects, and finally the "holy doctrines" themselves, and demonstrating, for those able to see, that all, absolutely all, are appearance only (purely phenomenal), and could not in any wise exist in their own right. The answer is left naked and obvious, and that is the "truth of Ch'an" (as of every other doctrine or non-doctrine which seeks to reveal it).

Someone may have perceived that people capable of apprehending the Supreme Vehicle were wasting their lives splitting logical and philosophical hairs, laboriously peeling off the leaves of the artichoke, cutting off the recrudescent heads of the hydra, instead of going straight to the heart *(hrdaya)* of the matter, and composed this admirable little "Sutra" which leaves the *hrdaya* revealed.

The *leit-motiv* of the whole composition is to turn people

away from their ceaseless objectivising, from their conditioned conceptualising, and, above all, from the illusory volition by means of which they imagine that they live and act,
so that, by turning their backs on what they are not, they may
suddenly become aware of the immensity of what they are.

Section II

But the message of the Sutra could rarely be revealed to us,
who have no Masters but books, expressed as it is, intentionally or otherwise, in objective terminology which turns the
mind away from the message that shines from its Heart.

In order to understand it we are required to bear in mind
that from beginning to end it is a description of the way in
which a *bodhisattva* sees, and that the speaking of the Sutra
is   itself   an   example   of   the   bodhisattvic-vision.
Avalokiteshvara, who speaks at the Buddha's command,
demonstrates to us how a *bodhisattva* perceives. He is not
informing us, as has usually been assumed, what the *skandha*
functions are or are not, or the phenomenal world which is
said to be sensorially perceived by their means. He is not
telling us yet again of the emptiness of objects as such. He is
telling us what they are—by revealing, and at the same time
demonstrating himself, that the well-known total lack of
being or own-nature of all that is objective is only an absence
objectively, and that such objective absence is itself the mind
of the *bodhisattva* and what he is. Therefore every line
expresses, not an objective concept but the perceiv*ing* or cog-
nis*ing* which is all that any *thing* ever was, is, or ever will be,
that is the pure *prajnaic* vision, direct, transcendent to conceptualisation, which is the functional aspect of what has
been called Dhyana.

This is most clearly stated in the Chinese text where

Avalokiteshvara says: "Sariputra, the voidness (of objective being) of all things has never been created and will never be destroyed, is neither composite nor pure, imperfect nor perfect." This is the "Void of Prajna," *Prajna* itself, and that is the key to the whole Sutra. It is a cursory but inclusive exposition of pure non-objective vision, of the transcendent subjectivity of a perfect *bodhisattva*. If *sunyata* be thought of just as sheer "emptiness," technically termed the "Void of Annihilation," rather than as the absence of objective being which is the *bodhisattvic* mind, the beating of the heart of the Heart Sutra can never be heard.

Note: Terms as use in Chinese Buddhism sometimes have a considerably different meaning from that they originally had in India. Buddhism was propagated in China largely via the technical terms and concepts of Taoism, which together with the considerably different philosophical attitude of the Chinese and Indians, resulted in radical differences of interpretation. Therefore what may be a fairly correct version of a Sutra translated from the Sanscrit may not be an accurate or even an adequate translation of the same Sutra as understood and used in China. As examples of terms to which this applies, *Samadhi, Sa-mo-di,* may be given, and perhaps *Prajna, Dhyana,* and several others, and as an example of a commoner concept, that implied by the word *sunyata* and its Chinese "equivalent" *k'ung,* which in Chinese Mahayana has the positive implication *wu-nien.*

In fact even if we have adequate knowledge of Mahayana Buddhism in India, it is with its development in China, as Ch'an— and the Japanese development of that, called Zen—and all the other Sects which constitute the Greater Vehicle, that we are concerned, for in China the practice of that survived and can be studied. The Supreme Vehicle particularly has to be recognised as an essentially Chinese creation, and that without loss of credit to its Indian inspiration and origin, but it is so deeply impregnated with Chinese philosophy and metaphysics that we cannot expect to be able to interpret and understand it on the sole basis of a literal Sanscrit translation.

I. A Rendering of the Sutra of the Divine Inseeing Mind Which Transcends Knowledge

Thus have I heard:

The Conqueror of Illusion[1] was on the Mount of Vultures, surrounded by a great concourse of monks and *bodhisattvas.* Rousing Himself from the state of *samadhi* in which He was plunged, after saluting the noble *bodhisattva* Avalokiteshvara, He asked him the following question: "What should be the vision of the son or daughter of a noble family[2] as a result of *prajna-paramita?*"[3]

Avalokiteshvara replied: A *bodhisattva* apperceives in this manner:

The Prajna-vision of a Bodhisattva

The five aggregates will be (cognised as) non-being.

Appearing will be (cognised as) non-being, and non-being will be cognised as Appearance.

---

[1] A name applied to the Buddha.

[2] Implying something like "member of the cultured classes"; here a *bodhisattva* is implied.

[3] Inseeing that transcends phenomenal knowledge; more lit. "hithershore subjectivity."

Appearing will be cognised as not-separate from non-being, and non-being as not-separate from Appearance.[1]

Perceiving will be cognised as non-being, and non-being will be cognised as Perception.

Perceiving will be cognised as not-separate from non-being, and non-being as not-separate from Perception.[1]

Thus also Conceiving, Conating, and being Conscious will be cognised, so that each will be apperceived as non-being, and non-being will be apperceived as each.[1]

In order to appreciate the above Section it is necessary to understand that the *bodhisattva*-vision is the subjective inseeing that is *Prajna*, which is the dynamic aspect of *Dhyana*, and that what is being taught is not the voidness, or even the nullity, of the *skandha* as objective faculties, but the subjectivity of the *bodhisattva*-vision, in which these conceptual objects have no being as such, but are identical subjectively with what is called "the void of *Prajna*," which may be defined as non-being regarding itself. In brief, the *skandha* have no objective being whatever, whereas what they are is subjective functioning of *Prajna*, exemplified in the very teaching being given here.

In fact, "voidness" or "emptiness" does not lie in any object whatever, but only, and entirely, in the cognising of it. The

---

[1] Apart from the one cognition there cannot be the other.

objects were never there to be "emptied," and nobody can empty (or fill), or otherwise affect, that which has no present existence. On the other hand, whatever the objects are said to be lies in their source—which is the noumenal *prajnaic* mind without whose dynamic action their phenomenal appearance could never have taken place.

Sariputra,[1] the vision of non-being (voidness of all objectivity) is uncreate and indestructible, neither composite nor pure, neither limited nor unlimited.

Thus Sariputra, in the *bodhisattva*-vision there can be no (reification of) Appearance or of Perception, of Conception, Conation or Consciousness.[2]

There can be no (reification of) eye or ear, nose or tongue, body or mind.[3]

There can be no reification of shape or sound, odour or savour, touch or concept.[4]

There can be no reification of the *objects* of seeing, of hearing, of smelling, of tasting, of touching, or of thinking.[5]

---

[1] A leading disciple of the Buddha.

[2] The five *skandha*, commonly regarded as objective faculties, but not here cognised *as such* (reified). Literally *a.* form, *b.* perceiving (form), *c.* conceptualising (form), *d.* conating (applied to form), *e.* knowing (conceptualised form).

[3] The six sense-organs.

[4] Their functions.

[5] Their phenomenal objects.

In the *bodhisattva*-vision *there can be no reification of
ignorance or* absence of ignorance; of decay and death or
absence of decay and death; of suffering, beginning or
end of suffering; of a "Way" ; of the knowledge, attainment or non-attainment of any object. [1]

This Section does not state that these objects, material or
conceptual, do not appear to exist phenomenally, nor even
that they do not exist otherwise than as appearance, but
merely that no events, no phenomena, no objective "things"
are present *as such* in the subjective vision of a *bodhisattva.*
In short, every imaginable thing may appear to exist phenomenally, but noumenally, in what can be described in philosophy as pure subjective mind, but which metaphysically can
only be indicated negatively as non-objectivity, no thing is,
was, or ever will be, and that is the *Prajna-vision* of a *bodhisattva.* In the final Section it is clearly stated.

> *Therefore, Sariputra, owing to the absence of Volition,
> and imbued with* prajnaparamita *(subjective inseeing)*,
> bodhisattvas *no longer are bound by interpretive thought-
> processes, and so have no fear, are freed from delusion, and
> have found* nirvana.

Whereas the first Section disposed of perceiving the
"being" of a phenomenal subject, by denying the "being" of

---

[1] The basic Buddhist doctrines, from the Four Noble Truths
onwards.

each of its faculties, the second Section disposed of perceiving the "being" of all the phenomenal objects of that subject, both psychic and somatic, including the doctrinal concepts of the *dhatu* (the eighteen sense-fields), the *nidana* (links in the chain of existence), the "Four Noble Truths," etc., by revealing their non-objective origin and source in all its implied noumenal sublimity.

In this third Section Avalokiteshvara indicates, with remarkable economy of expression, what this vision is, and to what it is due. We are so little used to such economy of verbiage in Indian Scriptures that the full value of each phrase may easily be overlooked. On examination it will be found that the one word "Volition" covers all ego-centred activities, whose absence is due to *prajnaparamita,* implying particularly here transcendence of conceptual thinking by means of direct perception antecedent to conceptualisation, of which absence the *bodhisattva's* noumenal living in perfect liberation, as described, is an inevitable consequence.

So it is that by means of "the *Prajnaparamita*" (the *mantram* so-called), all Buddhas, past, present and future, are fully awakened to *anuttara-samyak-sambhodi* (complete and perfect enlightenment).

Therefore we know that "the *Prajnaparamita*" is a great spiritual formula, an incomparable *mantram* which unfailingly makes an end of all suffering.

Then he uttered the true formula (invoking) *prajnaparamita,* which is:

"GATE, GATE PARAGATE, PARASAMGATE, BODHI
SVAHA!"

Note: As applied to the *mantram,* the title "the *Prajnaparamita*" probably implies just "formula of subjective transcendence." It gives the non-objective vision that is *Prajna,* whereby the resulting *bod-hisattva* lives directly without volitional interference.

Comment on This Famous Mantram

Few of us have much, if any, understanding of the use and potentiality of an Indian *mantram.** I submit these few lines for whatever they may be worth.

A *mantram* is not intended to be subjected to conceptual interpretation; therefore it need not be given in literal translation. It is not an exoteric *résumé* of doctrine, but an eso-teric—chiefly auditive—medium for the apperception of what universally we are. The indicative sense of these words might be rendered somewhat as follows, "Ah, *Bodhi!* (total subjective awareness or enlightenment), Welcome, welcome, well-come indeed—utterly 'ONE'!"

The sense usually given these six words, of *"Bodhi"* going further and further away, and finally landing up beyond the beyond, and then being "hailed," has no apparent significance. The alternative sense of the speaker's ego-self going away somewhere or other, and hailing *"Bodhi,"* seems scarcely more significant. *"Gate,"* either as "come" or as "go," seems dubious in any context here, for "who" or "what" can there be

---

* A perfect explanation was given by Ramana Maharshi when he stated "When a mantram is repeated, if attention is directed to the *source* whence the mantram-sound is produced, the mind is absorbed in that." The "absorption" of split-mind leaves its integrality intact. All the senses can fulfill this function, but particularly "hearing" and "seeing."

in this distillation of the pure doctrine of no-doctrine to "come" or to "go" any "where" or beyond "what"?

In a literal translation the sense of "fulfillment," instead of "displacement and arrival," can be carried by the Sanscrit words, as for instance, "accomplished, accomplished, fully accomplished, inseparably united! *Bodhi*, Svaha!" The exclamation is forever untranslatable into English.

II. In Technical Terms – I

Allow me now to give the elements of the Sutra in technical terms: this may clarify and confirm the interpretive rendering proposed above.

The Heart Sutra makes the following statements in all translations:

   i.   The five *skandha* are voidness.*

   ii.   Each of them is voidness, and voidness is each.

   iii.   Each is not separate from voidness, and voidness is not separate from each.

   iv.   Whatever each is, voidness is; and whatever voidness is, each is.

   v.   Voidness of all things is uncreate and indestructible.

   vi.   In voidness none of the five *skandha* exists.

   vii.   In voidness no thing (by inference, *produced* by them) exists.

   viii.   This is the way a *bodhisattva* sees (or understands); it

---

* The *skandha* too are the functional aspect of pure *prajnaic* non-objective mind.

is also that which has produced all Buddhas, and it is the *prajnaparamita.*

Note: Some translations of *v* state that everything being void-ness, no thing has any characteristics (attributes). The Chinese rendering, given above, is confirmed by the Commentary of the enlightened Master Han Shan.

Technically this means:

i. Five functional phenomena (appearances) are noumenon (their source).

ii. Each functional appearance is its source; its source is each functional appearance.*

iii. Each functional appearance is not separate from its source; its source is not separate from each functional appearance.

iv. Whatever each functional appearance is, its source is; whatever its source is, each functional appearance is.

v. Noumenon (source) is untouched by creation and destruction.

vi. In its source none of the functional appearances exists as an appearance.

vii. In the source of appearance no appearance of any kind (by inference, *produced* by the five functional appearances) exists.

viii. This is the way a *bodhisattva* sees (or understands); it is also that which has produced all Buddhas; and it is the *prajnaparamita.*

So presented, is it not evident?

Note: The familiar term "appearance" has been used for phenomenon, and "source" for noumenon.

PHENOMENA

ARE

NOTHING

BUT

NOUMENON

AND

NOUMENON

IS

ABSENCE

OF

NON-PHENOMENALITY

III. The Burden of the Heart Sutra - I

A Chinese Master said to me, "All Sutras are to teach people to 'empty.' . . . You cannot understand how to 'empty' before you understand the Heart Sutra." "To empty" is a Chinese way of saying "to see non-objectively whereby all things whatsoever, both objects and their subject, are devoid of any nature of their own," or "to rid 'seeing' of both subject and objects, whereby mind remains in its eternal purity."

Let me say it again in another form of words:

The question is not what *things* are or are not—as usually seems to be assumed to be the subject of this sutra, but how *things* are perceived by a bodhisattva (who sees as he should see).

The aim of the sutra, as appears evident on analysis, is to induce people to *see* correctly, instead of arguing about objects seen.

It is the seeing, and only the seeing, that matters: the emptiness or non-emptiness of the objects themselves is incidental, since that in any case depends exclusively on the seeing of them.

Hitherto interpretations of the Heart Sutra have tended to be concerned almost entirely with what objects are or are not, but it is evident that this is not the aim of the sutra, and that this preoccupation conceals its true message. The cause of this misconception lies in the versions of the text as we have it, which is expressed in objective terms, *nominal* instead of *verbal* parts of speech being used either deliberately or as the work of translators.*

---

* For example: "percep*tion*" instead of "appercei*ving*."

In short: the burden of the Heart Sutra is not the nature of objects as such, but the seeing of them—which is what they are, and the only nature they have.

IV. The Burden of the Heart Sutra - II

It does not appear to have been generally perceived that the apparently deliberate contradiction in the first and second paragraphs of the Heart Sutra is nothing of the kind.

Objective contradictions can never be resolved objectively, for no two concepts can ever be simultaneous, since they are extended in time. Not in a million *kalpas* can they be united, and no psychic or spiritual gymnastics, intuitions or anything else can ever reconcile them as phenomena. Intuition can only reveal the obvious, which is that in non-objectivity no contradiction remains.

Form and voidness (of form) can never be one as objects, but the perceiving of form and of voidness can indeed be identical, for it is *the perceiving itself,* not the apparently perceived, which is the same, and the perceiving is veritable whereas the perceived is only appearance, the one noumenon the other phenomena.

All objects are the perceiving of them, and the perceiving of them is what they are.

It follows that the perceiving of them is not separate from the objects, and the objects are not separate from the perceiving of them.

Therefore no objects exist as objects, either as phenomena or in noumenon.

The Heart Sutra teaches this as the vision of a bodhisattva, and it is the essential teaching of the Sutra.

Have we understood? What is called "voidness" is not an object, but a functioning. It is void because seeing cannot see seeing.

Appearing (form) is not an object, *but a functioning*. It appears as an objectivisation.

To "empty," therefore, is to apperceive non-objectively, void-seeing, no thing seen as such by no-see-er as such.

Doctrines also are ways of seeing, not things seen; they are not a description of absolute truths—for nothing of the kind could exist.

∽

All is just seeing: there is no *thing* seen.

And there is no see-er other than the seeing of the seen.

V. The Burden of the Heart Sutra - III

Voidness of Self and Other

The Heart Sutra is at once a description and a demonstration of the bodhisattvic vision by the Bodhisattva Avalokiteshvara, given at the request of the Buddha.

If a bodhisattva's vision were to perceive an object as such (as objectively existing), that object would thereby have a subject, that is to say that the bodhisattvic vision would have a subject as well as an object, and the bodhisattva whose vision it was would then no longer be a "bodhisattva."

Therefore in the bodhisattvic vision there can be neither subject nor object, neither see-er nor seen, but seeing only, just a seeing which is no seeing—for the bodhisattva is one with whatever he sees.

It follows that his seeing of form, which is object, is seeing of void, for appearance is void, and voidness here as always implies voidness of anything objective, and that is what, as a bodhisattva, he is. It follows also that seeing of voidness is seeing of form or appearance, for voidness which is the absence of anything seen when looking looks at looking, has no existence as such but only an apparent (phenomenal) existence when objectivised as form or appearance. The seeing of form is not separate from the seeing of void and *vice versa,* and whatever is seeing of form is seeing of void and *vice versa.*

It will now be obvious that sense-perceptions, the functional aggregates *(skandha),* and the dogmas (doctrinal elements) can have no objective existence in that voidness. They, too, are neither subject nor object, neither function nor the result of function, but functioning only.

Finally, "functioning" itself is void, and *voidness is "functioning."* Such is the bodhisattvic vision which is the burden of the Heart Sutra.

This can also be expressed in more technical language by stating that objects are their subject, and subject as such is each of its objects—for there is nothing that either could be but what mutually they are, whereas *in subject* no object can exist as such, and neither object nor subject exists objectively.

This bodhisattvic vision is common to all sentient beings: we are required to cognise in this manner, which is cognising as such in the *total absence of an objective cogniser and of any object cognised.* So doing, we are not, which is what we are.

Voidness of self and other—that is what mind is? Alas, no: voidness of self, other, and of mind also—that is the answer.

Note: The absence of an object entails the absence of its subject, but the "emptiness" of an object leaves the subject of that object intact. "Emptying" an object, therefore, is futile, for it is the absence of subject that is required. It is *mind as such* that must be "emptied" of both object and subject. Then there will be no "mind" either.

VI. *The Burden of the Heart Sutra - IV*

Perceiving - I

The Bodhisattvic perception is direct, immediate; that is to say, there has not yet intervened interpretation on the part of what is known as the sixth and seventh consciousnesses, i.e., the sixth "sense" (mano-vijñana) which coordinates the other five, and the intellectual consciousness (manas). Since these "consciousnesses" are discriminations, laboratory apparatus, invented in early India for analytical purposes, we are only required to refer to them or use them as such and not as objective existences.

Bodhisattvic perception is anterior to interpretation by any faculties whatever; therefore, *as perceived,* objects are not yet such: interpreted as this or that, they are still void (empty of objective character), in short they are not separated from void, nor made "different" by conceptualisation as external phenomena. Even if the normal process of objectivisation should be completed, so that the bodhisattva conceives the object in its inferential totality, he also perceives it for what it was, is, and ever will be, which intemporally and unextended in space is referred to as "void." This is the functioning called "prajna," which is a manner of indicating our non-objective "nature."

Note: This splitting of "mind" into perceived and perceiver brings into apparent existence, in inferred space and duration, objects and their subject; un-split "mind" is called (objectively) "void," its split and externalised condition is of the nature of phantasy, devoid of any character that is other than of the realm of thought. Its validity lies solely in the reunion of duality; i.e., the apparent objects are their subject, the subject is its apparent objects, the apparent existence of the latter being due to the splitting into "perceived" and "perceiver" thereof. It is pure experience where the bodhisattva is concerned—for he represents "mind" before it became divided, and before externalisation occurred.

Perceiving - II

Perceived objects are an externalisation of perceiving subject, subject itself objectified, the objective aspect of subject, as subject is the subjective aspect of object.

They are not different in any way, what each is the other is, they are not a "one" creating many, or many whose origin is "one."

Subject is no "thing" as subject—otherwise subject would be an object. Being no "thing," subject can have no attribute: the only form, colour, shape, size, or spatial character subject can have is *as object,* and the only absence of such attributes that object can know is as subject.

To make a concept of subject and object as two parts of a whole is to conceive two objects! Anything other than what you yourself are (what I myself am) is necessarily an object. Therefore subject must always be I, and I must always be everything which is to me an object, so that every single one of my objects is whatever I am.

What is this "whatever I am"? This is the great and apparent mystery which we find it so difficult to see through, precisely because we automatically identify subject with the object which others call by "our" personal name. If we could apperceive that subject is always and also object, and object always and also subject, we should be able profoundly to understand that neither could possibly have any independent existence as either, which, again, is the bodhisattvic vision wherein there is no see-er nor anything seen, but just a functioning that produces effects in what we know as consciousness. That, indeed, is freedom, for all bondage is limitation consequent on identification with a supposed object which could not exist as such. There is no other freedom, and it is liberation from all that is not joy.

All we are is that *whole* which manifests via "functioning," whose functioning splits *perceiving* into supposed perceiv*er* and supposed perceiv*ed*, which are two divisions extended in time, the perceiving and the perceived divisions in consciousness, wherein all phenomenal manifestation seems to occur as long as the two divisions are held apparently apart by the time-notion in function.

The bodhisattva's vision is pure "I-looking"—but that is Whole and has no objective quality or aspect.

VII. The Burden of the Heart Sutra - V

The Nonsense of Nullity

Chu Tao-ch'en (called Fa Shên, A.D. 286-374), one of a group of monks who studied and preached "Original Non-being," says "What is non-being? *An emptiness without shapes,* yet out of which the myriad things are engendered. Though the existent is productive, the non-existent has the power to produce all things."

On examination it will be found that the "non-existent," the "void," "non-being," etc., of which so much has been written and taught both before and since Fa Shên, in fact represents nothing whatever but a philosopher's attempt to objectify subjectivity.

Unless this is realised one will be tempted to try to conceive them objectively either as "inconceivable" annihilation and nothingness or as the equally "inconceivable" mysterious source and fountain-head of all things—an apparently contradictory alternative which, in fact, is not such at all.

However, the fact of endeavouring to conceive them as objects is itself simply looking in the wrong direction, for until the habitual mechanism of seeking to objectify every perception, to turn every percept into an objective concept, is abandoned, or laid aside in such contexts as these, the essential understanding cannot begin to develop.

We can see immediately that these so familiar emptinesses, variously described as "the non-existent, the void, non-being, etc." are not objects at all, can never be anything as objects, for they are what the perceiver of them is, and they can neither be seen to exist, to be, not to exist, or not to be—for they cannot be seen at all.

The perceiver in fact has arrived at a point in his investigation at which he is looking at what he is himself; he has reached a dead-end in his analysis and finds himself face to face with his own nature, but, instead of recognising it as such and realising that his void is what an eye sees when it looks at itself, he goes on trying to objectify what he does not see, what he can never see, by turning it into an objective concept, like the good and well-trained philosopher he usually is.

It seems likely that some knew this quite well, but, if so, they still persisted in the belief that there was no alternative to the objectifying process to which both they and their readers have been conditioned from infancy.

But there is, has always been, an alternative, when the dead-end, the *Ultima Thule* of conceptualisation has been reached, and that is just to turn round and wake up to the truth. Having arrived at the gate they tried to prise it open, not realising that they were already on the right side of it.

As concepts these notions of "non-being," "void," "non-existence," etc., are futile, useless and "empty" indeed: they merely indicate that the end of the road has been reached and that the traveller has only to turn round in order to find that he is already at his destination, which is home.

The sought is then seen to be the seeker.

VIII. Bodhisattvic Vision

The disturbing distinction between Nullity and the Absolute, between "the void of annihilation and the Void of Prajna," only has apparent validity in the conceptual (dualist) thought of subject-object. They are a pair of opposites, interdependent counterparts, like any other such pair, as, for instance, void and plenitude, emptiness and fullness, non-being and being, non-manifestation and manifestation. Playing with these on the *samsaric* level of divided mind creates a regrettable confusion that obstructs comprehension of the bodhisattvic vision, which is true seeing.

They represent the winding path of disposing of objects piece-meal as such, in order to dispose of the subject of each, instead of the direct path of the Supreme Vehicle (*Shresthyana*), the One Vehicle *(Ekyana)*, the Buddha Vehicle *(Buddhayana)* which stems directly from the source, and eliminates objects by the im-mediate elimination of their subject.

Phenomenally regarded, these opposites must always be separate and extended in time, for no two concepts could ever be simultaneously conceived, and psychological attempts to achieve this mystical union are just imaginative nonsense.

But in the direct bodhisattvic vision, which is available to every sentient being, there can be no difference between them. The inexistence of objects, objective nullity, absolute absence of form, of any "thing" sensorially or intellectually conceivable, total voidness and annihilation objectively, is identical with the Absolute, with Noumenon, with the source and origin of all manifestation, for in pure Perceiving there can be no "thing" seen, since there is no "thing" (object) that sees.

See-ing—being absolute suchness, this-ness, is-ness, here-ness, now-ness, unextended in space and duration, can know no subject-object differentiation between two concepts of divided mind which distinguishes two contradictory infer-ences such as manifestation and its source (called non-manifestation), being and non-being, form and void, fullness and emptiness.

Such concepts are just playing with words, verbal conjur-ing, terminological mystification, and, in fact—as you may observe—in most examples either term may be applied to either concept according to whichever notion you may choose to apply the concept of "real" and "unreal." For instance, is "being" phenomenal and "non-being" noumenal, or *vice versa?* To which do you apply the term "emptiness" and to which "fullness"? Are objects "void" or is "voidness" subject? Or are each both?

It could not matter, for each can be both, you can see either as either, both are concepts, and neither is at all in the bod-hisattvic vision, for their difference is merely conceptual inference on the part of divided mind functioning as subject and object.

Voidness which implies nullity, and voidness which implies the source of all phenomena, are not different, for each is a vision of total conceptual absence which is the only presence.

IX. *Omnipresence*

Everything that noumenally we are—is godhead-noumenon.

Everything that phenomenally we may be—is also god-head-noumenon.

Whatever godhead-noumenon (or noumenal godhead) may be—noumenally we are.

Whatever godhead-noumenon (or noumenal godhead) may be—phenomenally we are.

That is because no "thing" is, other than as objective phenomenon, which necessarily is the appearance, or manifestation, of noumenal godhead.

Noumenal godhead is every objective appearance, while whatever is not objective appearance is nothing but noumenal godhead.

There are no separate bits of noumenal godhead—for noumenal godhead is non-objectivity, which being the subjective source of conceptualisation, cannot be its object.

Therefore noumenal godhead knows no conceptual limitations, such as space-time.

Spaceless and timeless, there can be neither one (whole) nor parts.

There can only be *ubiquity*.

Note: May not this explain the Heart Sutra, spoken by a bodhisattva, telling how a bodhisattva apperceives? And is not the Heart Sutra said to contain the explanation of all that needs to be understood?

Part Four

❧

There is neither creation nor destruction,
Neither destiny nor free will,
Neither path nor achievement;
This is the final truth.

Sri Ramana Maharshi

It was true before he said it, it is true at this
moment, and it will be true forever, for there
is no time.

43 · The Resolution of Duality

THE CONCEPT of contraries is an effect of the concept of time: it is the result of a phenomenal extension of events in a context of duration, as, for instance, before and after, fast and slow, early and late.

It is also an effect of the concept of space: a result of phenomenal extension therein, as, for instance, left and right, up and down, long and short.

From the concept of space-time arise interdependent counterparts such as subject and object, positive and negative, *yin* and *yang,* alternating in time and separate in space.

Neither element of any pair of opposites or complementaries has any but a conceptual existence, and their resolution returns them to their source.

"Superimposed," each member of each pair of concepts annuls the other, and the result phenomenally is blank, and noumenally is non-being or non-manifestation, which is total absence as phenomenon, and total presence as noumenon.

That is the resolution of Duality.

Note: It is important to remember that sometimes a negative—such as non-being—is used not as the contrary of its positive, but in order to indicate the resultant of the mutual negation of each, neither the one nor the other, called also a double negative. It then implies noumenality.

This, of course, is the burden of the Diamond and Heart Sutras, of Padma Sambhava's Knowing the Mind, and the kernel of the doctrine of Hui Nêng and Shên Hui, in short of the Supreme Vehicle itself. It is the "understanding" that we are required not merely to subsume objectively, but to which subjectively we should be assumed. This subjective assumption involves a displacement of centre which results immediately in the bodhisattvic or prajnaic vision, whose essential characteristic is the cessation of automatic interpretive objectivisation, and the substitution of direct non-volitional apperceiving.

44 ·- *Shadows*

WHAT IS called "identification" is that effect of conditioning whereby a shadow is taken for its substance, the source of the shadow, and all they both are, whether united or apparently separated in the dimensions of space.

It might almost be possible to say that not only is shadow taken for substance, but also that substance—if cognised at all—is taken for shadow.

But a shadow has no life of its own, nor any nature, character, or attribute; all it is lies in its source, of which it is a phenomenal reflection, deformed, partial, limited to two dimensions, constantly in flux, and utterly devoid of entity, an abstraction, an "appearance" illusorily separated from its own substance.

However, everything the shadow appears to do, its every manifestation, as it is perceived is not performed by its substance but is an objectified representation of some movement on the part of that source.

Sentient phenomena likewise lack the essential dimension of their source, and are appearances illusorily separated from their substance—which is the noumenon which is all that they are.

45 ·— *Seeing, Seeing, Seeing . . .*

WHAT IS the use of looking outside? All you will see is objects! Turn round and look within.

Shall I then see subject instead?

If you did you would be looking at an object. An object is such in whatever direction you look.

Shall I not see myself?

You cannot see what is not there!

What, then, shall I see?

Perhaps you may see the absence of yourself, which is what is looking. It has been called "the void."

Boomerang

Every time you see an object you are beholding the subject of that object in its objective manifestation.

Every object is a mirror which reflects what is looking.

46 ·— *The Illusion of Enlightenment*

IF YOU have the basic understanding that the primal Buddha-nature is that of all sentient beings, it follows that anyone who thinks that any *action* can lead to his "enlightenment" is turning his back on the truth: he is thinking that there is a "he" there to be "enlightened," whereas "enlightenment" is a name for the state wherein there is no separate individual at all, and which is that of all sentient beings, a name for what they are, but which cannot be recognised by anyone who believes himself to be an autonomous individual.

That is why only the action of non-action, the practice of non-practice, unmotivated non-volitional functioning, can lead to that recognition or awakening, and why any kind of action, practice or intentional procedure is an unsurmountable barrier to such awakening.

The error depends on the rooted superstition of the existence as such of an individual being.

This may be more obvious if you say that no *phenomenon* could be enlightened, since enlightenment is not phenomenal: it is just noumenon.

That which is not phenomenal in a sentient being, described above as the "primal Buddha-nature," needs no "enlightenment"—since that is precisely what it is.

Note: "Action" which implies "effort" implies "intention," which is Volition, which is the functional aspect of an I-concept. It should not be difficult to perceive that such "action" could not result in awakening *from identification with*—an I-concept!

"Awakening" is awakening to the immutable enlightened state.

"Unmotivated non-volitional functioning," mentioned in par. 2 above, as a continuous manner of "being lived" is *a result of* awakening rather than a "method" or "practice" to that end. It is also the Way itself, the way of living in the sense of Tao.

47 ◦ *Grammatically Speaking*

FROM A PRACTICAL point of view one of the chief hindrances to our understanding of the message of the Masters lies simply in the parts-of-speech used in delivering their teaching. In brief, nouns are used where the meaning can only be suggested by verbs.

Modern translators are not by any means entirely to blame, though ultimately the fault lies in lack of understanding on the part of all the intermediaries concerned. The Buddha himself spoke in Maghadi, and his teaching was recorded many years later in Pali and in Sanscrit. Few of our authorities left anything in writing, and what we have of theirs has passed through many hands before reaching us. Indian *Mahayana* moved out of India long centuries ago, and it is the development and practice of it in China which we can study, and in the written language of China parts-of-speech are practically non-existent. Finally modern languages, particularly French with its Cartesian tradition, are deeply rooted in objective forms, so that it is difficult, and sometimes impossible, to express any thought otherwise than in a purely objective manner. But the essence of the message of the Masters is precisely that what is objectivised is not true as such, and that what we are can only be apprehended by ceasing to "apperceive" like that.

As long as nouns are used for the expression of a teaching, that teaching is dealing with objects as such, whether the objects be physical or mental, but the burden of the teaching can only be conveyed by the use of adverbial forms and by verbs, for the teaching is concerned with functioning rather than with anything nominal that functions, or with anything nominal that results from functioning, both of which are purely inferential. This applies to every aspect of the teaching. For instance Time and Space are not to be thought of as "things"; as nouns we misunderstand them at once, for they are at most adjectival—that is, dependent on the functioning that makes use of them as concepts. And the "skandha," the senses, the various conceptualised sorts or degrees of consciousness, are all functioning—and can only be expressed as verbs, or as dependent, adverbially. As objects the teaching is that they have no existence whatever.

Even so, the expression is necessarily imperfect, for it is axiomatic that any truth, including truth itself, cannot be expressed at all, but can only be suggested or indicated, for conceptually there can be no truth. The essential fact is that the use of nouns points directly in the opposite direction to that which could suggest or indicate, and thereby nullifies the teaching being presented, and makes sheer nonsense of it, whereas the use of adverbial and verbal parts-of-speech admits suggestion and indication as directly as can ever be possible. With nominal expression misunderstanding is inevitable, and at best readers persuade themselves that they have glimpsed a technically impossible amalgamation of contradictions-in-terms, whereas with verbal expression non-objective cognition immediately becomes feasible.

48 ·– Whose Mind?

NEXT TIME we hear someone talking about "his" mind or "yours," let us ask who there could possibly be to possess such an article! Huang Po, in the ninth century in China, and Sri Ramana Maharshi eleven centuries later, both replied in the same words, in their respective languages, to a visitor who produced such a notion: their words, ironical and full of humour, were just this: "How many minds *have* you?"

In the Tun Huang Cave there was found a MS of a number of sayings of Bodhidharma recorded by his disciples. One of them runs as follows: "What is the Buddhamind?" and Bodhidharma's reply, "It is your (only) mind. When you apperceive it subjectively it can be called Suchness. When you apperceive its immutability it can be called Dharmakaya. It is not any thing, so it may be called Liberation. Its functioning is imperceptible, undisturbed by any object, so it may be called pure Tao. Never born, it can never die, so it may be equated with Nirvana." It is not "your" mind, of course: "you"—all you could be—are what it is.

Whoever Bodhidharma may have been—other than a monk of the Lanka sect, wherever he may have "lived," or even if he did not, are not the words attributed to him clearly the essential revelation?

Note: We are all incessantly familiar with its objectified reflection in phenomenal life, but its non-objective nature is *wu-nien*, which can never be objectivised as conscious*ness*.

49 ⏀ In Technical Terms – II

The Apparent Mystery

PHENOMENA, AS phenomena, cannot be the source of phenomena; nevertheless, since they cannot be anything but their noumenon, ultimately they are one with their source.

Therefore as objects we cannot be anything but appearance, but as objects we are not the subject of our appearance; nevertheless since there is nothing that we could be as objects other than our subject, ultimately we are one with our subject.

That subjective noumenon, however, is necessarily transcendent, is devoid of objective being, and therefore cannot be regarded even as "one."

That is why phenomenally, as it is said, we "are not"; i.e., we are appearance only, and why, noumenally we "are not" either, as "us," that is as objects, for noumenally we are subject and, as such, "are not" as objects.

So, as it is said, *we* "neither are nor are not" because there never was any "we," other than as an objective appearance, to be, and so *what we are* is the absence of both concepts.

How simple and obvious it becomes when expressed in the terms to which we are used!

I Am—but There Is No "I"

As long as we believe that what we are is an object—the idea of an "I" will always be present.

But whenever we apperceive that what we are cannot be an object—the idea of "an I" will necessarily be absent.

For the idea of an "I" is itself a conceptual object, and nothing that is objective could be this which we are.

Definition of Non-objective Relation

There is neither objective self nor objective other, but only this mutual absence, which is what noumenally we are.

Where no concept of separation is present there can be no affectivity. There is no longer relation either, but wholeness instead. And "wholeness" is cognate with healing and "holiness," and the pure joy of non-affectivity is implicit therein.

50 ·– Saying It Even More Simply

Every perceptible "thing" is a product of mind.
What we are as "things" is that,
And what we are otherwise than as "things" is that also.

Every manifestation, then, is a product of mind.
Whatever we may be as manifestation is a product of
    mind.
Whatever we may be otherwise than as what is manifested
Is mind itself.

Since mind is only manifest in manifestation,
Itself is non-manifestation.

So that is what we are otherwise than as manifested.
Thus we, sentient beings, are mind itself manifesting,
And, objectively, mind manifesting as "things."

Noumenon, as the term states, is mind.
Phenomenon, as the term states, is appearance.
Unmanifested, we are noumenon,
Manifested, we are appearance (phenomenon).

They are not separate, no more separate than substance
and its form.
Their difference is in appearance, which one has and the
other has not.
Why is that?
Because, in manifesting, mind divides into observer and
observed.
That which is observed is appearance,
Its observer is the counterpart of appearance,
Dual aspects of manifesting mind.

Knowing that the observed has no existence
Apart from the observer,
Knowing that the observer has no existence
Apart from the observed,
Divided mind is re-united.

Then there is no other, so there can be no self.
Then there is no self, so there can be no other.
Without extension in space, without duration in time,
In mind that is whole,
There is no being to suffer, to experience pain or pleasure,
To hate or to love.

Gone with its ego, the scourge of volition,
Mind as a concept, utterly absent,
Pure noumenality, none to conceive it,
Untrammelled and radiant, is all that we are.

51 · Disillusion

Perceiving a coil of rope as a snake, is delusion;
Ceasing to perceive a snake, leaves the perceiving of the
    coil of rope what it is.
Perceiving a coil of rope as a coil of rope, is still delusion.
Ceasing to perceive a coil of rope as a coil of rope, leaves
    the perceiving of the supposed coil of rope whatever the
    supposed coil of rope may be.
Whatever the supposed coil of rope may be is *devoid* of the
    concept of a coil of rope,
Because voidness is perceiving perceiving itself,
For the perceiver of the snake-perception, and of the rope-
    perception, must go with its objects, leaving perceiv*ing*
    only—which is what is, or suchness.

Identity

Emptiness, which is nullity (no form), which is
    noumenon, which is subject, which is self,
And plenitude, which is appearance (form), which is phe-
    nomenon, which is object, which is other,
Are inseparable, are aspects one of another, are interde-
    pendent counterparts.
Mutually contradictory as concepts of divided-mind, at
    their source in whole-mind, anterior to conceptual dual-
    ity, in the absence of objective interpretation,
Their identity is absolute.

We are required to perceive, and to understand, that their objective interpretation as opposites is delusion, and that their absolute identity is disillusion—which is awakening from all illusion.*

By comprehending that an object is always, inevitably, its subject—for what else could it be?—that other must always be self, phenomenon noumenon, appearance nullity (its non-objective source), and plenitude the emptiness of the Absolute, this identity of conceptual contraries becomes evident.

That is why delusion and disillusion (sometimes called Ignorance and Enlightenment) are the same and, when perceived as such, it is the "enlightened" mind (whole mind) which is perceiving.

Being that, the perceived is the perceiver—and the course is run.

52 ∙– Let Us Do This

By jointly discussing noumenon and phenomenon, one reaches the highest consciousness and creates right understanding among sentient beings. This is called the theory of relying on phenomenal things in order to elucidate truth.

FA TSANG, A.D. 643-712, in "The Gold Lion"

---

* Who is "required to understand"? Our noumenality requires: our phenomenality *appears* to perceive and to understand; but only *understanding* is, and we are that.

Fa Tsang was the founder of the Hua Yen Sect, based on the Avatamsaka Sutra, philosophically the most evolved form of Buddhism, and, perhaps, completing the doctrine of the Wei Shih Sect, founded by the famous monk who travelled to India, Hsüan Tsang, A.D. 596-664, with whom he worked for some years. Both Sects survive to-day. The Hua Yen Sect, is sometimes called the "Garland of Flowers Sect," which is the meaning of *Avatamsaka,* called Kegon in Japan. The Wei Shih Sect is called the "Pure Consciousness Sect," and, philosophically, the "Mere Ideation School."

The advice is sound, and the source of the advice unimpeachable.

There is no phenomenon without noumenon, and no noumenon without phenomenon.

There is no subject without objects, and there are no objects without subject.

There is no separate "one" outside of the "many," nor "many" outside of the "one."

This is an aspect of the same doctrine, though indeed it speaks for itself.

"Once we have reached enlightenment, the illusory itself becomes the real, so that no other reality remains." —*Fa Tsang,* "Hua Yen Huan-yüan Kuan"

Before Awakening, "others-and-self are differingly felt,

non-being-and-being are differently perceived"; Awakened, "things and self are equally forgotten (both eliminated), being and non-being are viewed in one and the same way."

"The equating of non-being and being, others and self, leads to Enlightenment." (Hsieh Ling-yün, also called Hsieh Yung-chia A.D. 385-433, in his "Discussion of Essentials")

Here Hsieh Yung-chia is recording and discussing the words of the great Tao Shêng *(c.* A.D. 360-434), founder of Ch'an Tsung in China some three generations before the assumed dates of Bodhidharma. Tao Shêng, together with the group of monks, of whom the best-known are Sêng Chao (A,D. 374-414) whose *Book of Chao* has been translated by Walter Liebenthal—a student, with Tao Shêng, of Kuma-rajiva, and Hsieh Yung-chia (A.D. 385-433), elaborated the doctrine subsequently known as Ch'an, in Japan as Zen, and gave it a perfection of simple expression which in that respect was never equalled by any of the later masters.

It will be observed that the teaching emphasises at once that the question is one of perceiv-*ing*, via split-mind on the part of the identified, by whole-mind by the awakened. This again is the Bodhisattvic Vision dealt with elsewhere. Things, facts, objects, expressed as nouns, simply are not, all is function-*ing* and the truth can only be indicated, in so far as that can ever be done, by using verbal forms of speech for what is usually translated for us by nouns, such as the meaningless "wisdom" and so many other misleading terms.

"Here we find a combination of Taoist and Buddhist ideas. What we call 'retribution' results from the activity of the mind. Our aim, therefore, should be to respond to external situations *without interposing the mind,* since such a course permits physical activity, yet involves *no mental activation.* This is the way to transcend the cycle of trans-migration, so that our acts no longer entail any retribution."

That is *spontaneous response without volitional activity.*

The above is Fung Yu-lan's comment on "The Explanation of Retribution" by Hui Yüan (A.D. 334-416, founder of the Pure Land Sect) which is presumed to embody the teaching of a lost work of Tao Shêng on that subject. "Retribution" implies what is now known as "karma."

The Taoist elements in Chinese Buddhism are very precious. There has never been, to my knowledge, in the West a man of Tao who has revealed this teaching in a European language, nor a translator who has fully understood it, and indeed surely more nonsense has been written about so called "Taoism" than about any other "religion" on earth.

Yet it is supreme in its grandiose simplicity and, as far as I am aware, lacks nothing essential that later doctrines have supplied. It may be called the religion beyond religion, and the basis of whatever can be called truth in any metaphysical doctrine. Its survival in the higher reaches of Buddhism, in which it is integral, is still its most accessible form and their own most essential element.

In the observation quoted, objection may be taken to the word "aim." Indeed it might be happier if one said "Our understanding, therefore, should respond to external situations without interference."

Note: In two quotations above I have left the misleading term "enlightenment." Since, however, that is the timeless nature of all sentient beings, it cannot be reached, led to, or otherwise attained, but translators *will* use it thus despite the endless reminders of the great masters as to what it means. The phrase in each case should be "reach, or lead to, *Awakening,*" or *"awakening* to enlightenment."

॰৵

Fung Yu-lan's summing up of the doctrine of Ch'an is noteworthy, for his scholarship is all-embracing, he is outstanding among living Chinese philosophers, and his metaphysical insight is clearly exceptional.

After pointing out that alternative interpretations exist concerning the meaning of *wu*, translated as "nonbeing," the one implying nullity, the other implying the mind from which all things arise, he suggests that Sêng Chao accepted the first interpretation, and Tao Shêng the second, the later differentiation being between the doctrine enunciated as "not mind, not Buddha" (or "neither mind nor Buddha"), and "being mind, being Buddha" (or, "both mind and Buddha"). I have pointed out, however, that both interpretations are identical, and perhaps sufficiently explained why they must be identical, in the vision of a bodhisattva. (p. 91)

Then he sums up as follows: "All Ch' anists, however, irrespective of which interpretation they accept, emphasise five main points:*

  i. The Highest Truth or First Principle is inexpressible;
  ii. Spiritual cultivation cannot be cultivated;
  iii. In the last resort nothing is gained;
  iv. There is nothing much in the Buddhist teaching;
  v. In carrying water and chopping wood: therein lies the wonderful Tao;" (i.e., non-volitional living).

---

* In illustration of each of these five points he devotes a short section of citation and discussion which constitute probably the most penetrating and perspicacious delineation of Ch'an at present available—*History of Chinese Philosophy*, vol. ii, p. 390-406, Princeton, 1953

53 · Seeing It Simply

IT IS surely axiomatic that a phenomenon (an appearance, an object) cannot perform any action whatever on its own initiative, as an independent entity. In China this was illustrated by Chuang Tzu in his story of the sow who died while suckling her piglets: the little pigs just left her because their mother was no longer there. In Europe, even at that early date, the same understanding is expressed by the word *animus* which "animates" the phenomenal aspect of sentient beings, and this forms the basis of most religious beliefs. But whereas in the West the "animus" was regarded as personal to each phenomenal object, being the sentience of it, in the East the "animus" was called "heart" or "mind" or "consciousness," and in Buddhism and Vedanta was regarded as impersonal and universal, "Buddha-mind," "Prajna," "Atman," etc.

When this impersonal "mind" comes into manifestation by objectifying itself as subject and object, it becomes identified with each sentient object, and the concept of "I" thereby arises in human beings, whereby the phenomenal world as we know it and live it, appears to be what we call "real." That, incidentally, is the only "reality" (thing-ness) we can ever know, and to use the term "real" (a thing) for what is not such, for the purely subjective, is an abuse of language.

In this process of personalising "mind" and thinking of it as "I," we thereby make it, which is subject, into an object, whereas "I" in fact can never be such, for there is nothing objective in "I," which is essentially a direct expression of subjectivity. This objectivising of pure subjectivity, calling it "me" or calling it "mind," is precisely what constitutes "bondage." It is this concept, termed the I-concept or ego or self, which is the supposed bondage from which we all suffer and from which we seek "liberation."

It should be evident, as the Buddha and a hundred other Awakened sages have sought to enable us to understand, that what we are is this "animating" mind as such, which is noumenon, and not the phenomenal object to which it gives sentience. This does not mean, however, that the phenomenal object has no kind of existence whatever, but that its existence is merely apparent, which is the meaning of the term "phenomenon"; that is to say, that it is only an appearance in consciousness, an objectivisation, without any nature of its own, being entirely dependent on the mind that objectivises it, which mind is its only nature, very much as in the case of any dreamed creature, as the Buddha in the Diamond Sutra, and many others after him have so patiently explained to us.

This impersonal, universal mind or consciousness, is our true nature, our only nature, all, absolutely all, that we are, and it is completely devoid of I-ness.

This is easy enough to understand, and it would be simple indeed if it were the ultimate truth, but it is not, for the obvious reason that no such thing as an objective "mind" could exist, any more than an "I" or any other object, as a thing-in-itself. What it is, however, is totally devoid of any objective quality, and so cannot be visualised, conceptualised, or in any way referred to, for any such process would automatically render it an object of subject—which by definition it can never be. That is because the "mind" in question is the unmanifested source of manifestation, the process of which is its division into subject and object; and antecedent to such division there can be no subject to perceive an object, and no object to be perceived by a subject. Indeed, and as revealed by sages such as Padma Sambhava, *that* which is seeking to conceive and to name this unmanifested source of manifestation is precisely *this* "whole mind" which is the "animating" or "prajnaic" functioning which *itself is the seeking,* so that the sought is the seeker thereof.

Profoundly to understand this is Awakening to what is called "enlightenment."

This reasoned visualisation, therefore, like all doctrine, is merely conceptual, devoid of factuality, a structure of theoretical imagination, a symbolical diagram devised in order to enable us to understand something immediate that can never become knowledge. Yet that ultimate "something," which is no "thing," is nevertheless what the universe is, and all that we are.

The psychological "I-concept" has no nature of its own, is no "thing," and could not possibly create genuine "bondage." There cannot be any such thing as bondage at all, but only the idea of such. There is no liberation, for there is no "thing" from which to be freed. If the whole conceptual structure is seen as what it is, it must necessarily collapse, and the bondage-enlightenment nonsense with it. That is called Awakening, awakening to the natural state which is that of every sentient being. Sri Ramana Maharshi taught just that when he said that "enlightenment" is only being rid of the notion that one is not "enlightened," and Maharshi might have been quoting the T'ang dynasty Chinese sage Hui Hai, known as the Great Pearl, when he stated that Liberation is liberation from the notion of "liberation." He might also have been quoting Huang Po *(d. 850),* of whom he is unlikely ever to have heard, when they both used the same words, full of humour, to someone asking about "his" mind: each sage asked in reply, "How many minds *have* you?"

How many minds had they, those two young men? Why, none at all. Not only not two, but not one. Nor were they themselves a "mind," for there could not be such a thing as a "mind" for them to be. Neither "they" nor "mind" ever had, or ever could have, any objective being whatever, for never has

111

any kind of objective being *been,* nor will such ever *be.* All that, and every "that" which ever was thought up—and "that" is the most purely objective of pronouns—is the essence of the gigantic phantasmagoria of objectivity, which we spend our lives building up, and in which we search desperately for some "truth" which could not possibly be there. The whole vast construction is a phantasy, a dream, as the Buddha (or whoever wrote it in his name) told us in the Diamond Sutra, and the truth which a dream represents, or misrepresents, of which it is a reflection or a deflection, is the dreaming source of it which is all that it is. That source can never have a name, because a name denotes a phenomenon—and there is no phenomenal dreamer, but a function*ing* that is called dream-*ing*. Sri Bhagavan called it "I-I": if it must be called anything, no nominal form could ever come nearer, or be less mislead-ing as an indication, than his term.

All objectivisation is conceptual, all conceptuality is infer-ence, and all inference is as empty of truth as a vaccum is empty of air. Moreover there is no truth, never has been and never could be; there is no thusness, suchness, is-ness, nor anything positive or negative whatever. There is just absolute absence of the cognisable, which is absolute presence of the unthinkable and the unknowable—which neither is nor is not. Inferentially this is said to be an immense and radiant splendour untrammelled by notions of time and space, and utterly beyond the dim, reflected sentience of temporal and finite imagination.

54 ⸗ *The Essential Identity*
(Without Sanscrit or Chinese technical terms)

I

"POSITIVE" IS not positive without "negative," and "negative" is not negative without "positive." Therefore they can only be two halves of one whole, two conceptual aspects of one whole which as a whole cannot be conceived—precisely because it is this which seeks to conceive.

"Being" cannot *be* without "non-being," and "nonbeing" cannot *not be* without "being." Therefore they can only be two conceptual aspects of one whole which as such cannot be conceived—in which there is neither being nor non-being as objective existences.

"Appearance" (form) cannot appear without "void" (voidness of appearance), and "void" cannot be voidness of appearance without "appearance." Therefore they must be two conceptual aspects of what is objectively inconceivable—as which their identity is absolute in non-objectivity.

"Subject" has no conceptual existence apart from "object," nor "object" apart from "subject." They, too, are twin spinning aspects of the inconceivable in which they are inevitably reunited in mutual negation.

Where there is neither positive nor negative, being nor non-being, appearance nor void, subject nor object, there must be identity. But identity cannot perceive itself, and that is what we are. That is why only he who does not know can speak, and why he who knows cannot speak—for what-he-is cannot be an object of what-he-is, and so cannot be perceived or described.

Positive and negative, being and non-being, appearance and void, subject and object, can be conceived by us because, as "us," mind is divided into subject-conceiving and object-conceived but, re-identified with what they are, we are their total objective absence—which is thought of as pure undivided mind.

"Space" is a static three-dimensional concept, of which "time" is the active counterpart, whose functioning constitutes a further direction of measurement. Space cannot be conceived without time (duration), nor time without space (extension). Two conceptual aspects of a unity which is inconceivable; given the name of "space-time," their identity is absolute in non-conceptuality. Unaccompanied by them, phenomena cannot be extended in appearance, and only with space-time as their noumenal source can phenomena be assumed to be.

"Phenomena" cannot be such without "noumenon," nor "noumenon" without "phenomena." Therefore conceptually they also are two aspects of non-conceptuality. Phenomena, being no things in themselves (devoid of self-nature) yet are everything, and noumenon, being the source of everything, yet is no thing. Everything, then, is both, and neither is any thing: eternally separate as concepts, they are forever inseparable unconceived, and that identity is the essential understanding.

That is what the universe is in so far as its nature can be suggested in words. The universe is inconceivable, because what it is, is what we are, and what we are is what the universe is—and that is total absence cognitionally which, uncognised, necessarily subsists as total presence.

"By jointly discussing noumenon and phenomenon, one reaches the highest consciousness and creates right understanding among sentient beings"—*Fa Tsang*, A.D. 642-712, founder of the Hua Yen Sect of Buddhism, based on the *Avatamsaka Sutra*

II

We cannot use mind to transcend mind: therefore noumenon (which is the abstract of mind) represents the limit of possible cognition.

"Noumenon" necessarily is total potentiality. If it functions, in functioning it must be subjective, and thereby inevitably objective also. That is to say, subject objectivises itself and so becomes apparent to itself as object, manifesting phenomenally "within" itself. It looks at itself and perceives the universe—which is then apparently outside itself, since objectivisation is a process of apparent exteriorisation.

Therefore the phenomenal universe is the objective aspect of noumenon.

This process comports the appearance of space and duration without which objects could not have the necessary extension—and without their extension there could be no cognition.

Phenomena, therefore, are not something projected by noumenon: they are *the appearance of noumenon*—or noumenon rendered objective and apparent.

This function-ing is what sentient beings are, and, *that* extension in space-time is what we know as manifestation. In *that* appearance—like all phenomena, of which our appearance is an aspect—we have no nature of our own, but in *this* function-ing (which is our nature) *noumenality and phenomenality are identical.*

This is why, thus manifested, *we are not as such* (phenomenally), and why *we are* as phenomenal noumenality (or noumenal phenomenality). Thus there is no duality in what we are, but only an apparent autonomous function-ing which is the manifesting of non-manifestation.

No entity is involved in what we are, for "entity" is a

phenomenal concept—and every object, material or conceptual, that is phenomenal, is devoid of nature *(is* not). When the autonomous functioning, which is all that we are in manifestation, no longer functions—i.e., when it no longer extends itself in an apparent space-time continuum, this-which-we-are remains totally integrated in noumenality.

Noumenality as such cannot be recorded. What "noumenality" represents neither is nor is not. It is necessarily incognisable, because totally devoid of objective quality, as "mirrorness" is, and because it is precisely what we are, and absolutely all that we are, whether non-manifested or in apparent manifestation.

Let the final word be with Huang Po: "There is no difference between sentient beings and Buddhas, or between Samsara and Nirvana, or between delusion and *bodhi*. When all such forms are abandoned there is the Buddha."

55 ⸱⁓ *Observations Concerning Causation*

Only That Which Is Objective Can Be Bound

ONLY THAT which is objective can be dependent upon the law of causation, can be an effect of cause, or can experience the effect of causes.

The process of cause-effect is dependent on time (duration) and necessarily is phenomenal; therefore every phenomenon must be dependent on temporal causation.

That which is dependent on causation, being the result of causes, no volitional element can interfere with the operation of this process, and there can not be any entity therein to exercise "freedom of will."

On the other hand non-objectivity can never be dependent

on causation, and, not being phenomenal, can never be bound, or ever suffer any experience.

Moreover whatever is non-objective cannot be an entity (which is an objective concept), and so there cannot be any noumenal exercise of volition either, and there can be no "will" to be bound or to be free.

Volition (acts of "will"), therefore, necessarily are illusory; they can only be an apparent interference in the operation of causality which inevitably is ineffectual.*

Thus "purpose" and "intention" on the part of an imaginary entity can only find fulfillment or frustration when they are in accordance with, or in opposition to, an effect of causation, and such frustration or fulfillment can only be

---

* The idea that the exercise of volition on the part of a phenomenal object could introduce a new cause into the apparently inexorable chain of causation, and new causes on the occasion of every such exercise, could only imply the existence of an objective entity operating subjectively with "freedom of will."

Theoretically this is as impossible as it is contrary to the basic teaching of the Buddha so frequently reiterated in the Diamond Sutra and elsewhere. Yet it appears to be implicit in the teaching of all the more limited and popular forms of Buddhism.

Evidently, however, it is not any such inconceivable intervention that is in question, and that is said to create *karma* thereby. What is mistaken for such is a psychic impulsion conceptualised as "purpose" or "intention," expressed as volition, in accordance with, or in opposition to, whatever event necessarily must take place, or not take place as a result of cause-and-effect, thereby producing either fulfillment or frustration which is the psychological basis of the "karmic" idea.

psychological phenomena.

This is the meaning of *yu-wei* and *wu-wei*. The former implies attempted volitional action on the part of a pseudo-entity, that which self-identified sentient beings regard as every action they perform, apart from those over which they cannot claim or pretend any control—such as the circulation of the blood, or digestion.

The latter, *wu-wei*, implies every effective action "they" appear to perform as a result of causes antecedent in "time," regardless of any attempted volitional interference with such action, as of the absence of any such attempted interference. The former is conventionally indicated as phenomenal or "false" action, the latter as non-phenomenal or "true" action. For example, a sentient being eats because nourishment is needed as an effect of physiological causation, or it falls asleep because sleep is similarly required, whether it *wishes* or purposes to do so or not to do so; and the *desire* or intention so to do, or not so to do, is a psychological phenomenon that cannot appear to be effectual unless it is in accord with antecedent causes.

The notion of causes being antecedent, however, may be questioned, for there appears to be no valid reason to suppose that causes, although dependent on the time-factor, are necessarily anterior to their effects; that is to say, it is conceivable that effects may precede some of their causes which thus may be posterior in "time" (still in the future) to the moment of the effectual occurrence. Probable as this may be, it should not materially effect the apparent operation of causality.*

---

* Whatever appears to occur must conform with whatever must occur later in the time-sequence (in the future).

Voiding of all *that* which is objective does not leave an object which voids or is voided. There is just no "thing" of any kind, physical or psychic, therein. Thus in what has been referred to as "non-objectivity" there can be no entity, and therefore no volition, nor any causation—for therein can be no thing to be caused, so that all these notions are seen to be merely phenomenal concepts.

This which can only be suggested as pure voiding of objectivity is the pure functioning of *prajna.*

56 ⁓ For Síle

I

When the beetle sees, it is I that am looking,
When the nightingale sings, it is I that am singing,
When the lion roars, it is I that am roaring.

But when I look for myself, I can see nothing—for no thing is there to be seen.
Síle cannot see me either, for when she tries to see me it is I who am looking: she can do nothing—for only I can do anything.
The beetle can say that also, and Síle, for we are not three, nor two, nor one.

I am the sea too, and the stars, the wind and the rain,
I am everything that has form—for form is my seeing of it.
I am every sound—for sound is my hearing of it,
I am all flavours, each perfume, whatever can be touched,
For that which is perceptible is my perceiving of it,
And all sentience is mine.

119

They have no other existence, and neither have I—for
  what they are I am, and what I am they are.
What the universe is I am, and what I am the universe is.
And there is no *other* at all, nor any *one* whatsoever.
Gate, gate, paragate, parasamgate, Bodhi! Svaha!

II

Although such manifestations as hurricanes and tornados,
floods and tidal-waves, are destructive in character, disagreeable phenomena may seem to have been ignored in the
foregoing. The phenomenally destructive aspect of pure
functioning may be presented somewhat as follows.

A cat plays with and eats a mouse, a lion kills and devours
an antelope,

A sportsman shoots and dines off a pheasant, a cannibal
cooks and feasts on a missionary,

A soldier drops an atomic bomb and annihilates ten-
thousand sentient beings.

By the perpetrators: the cat, the lion, the sportsman, the
cannibal, the soldier, this functioning is interpreted as "good."

By the victims: the mouse, the antelope, the pheasant, the
missionary, and the bombed, this functioning is interpreted
as "evil."

To each, each deed *appears* to be his deed, or his experience,
but none can perform any deed, or suffer any experience, for
no phenomenal object has any independent existence of its
own. And there is no judge.

I alone am the functioning that is thus manifested—and
all sentient beings can say these same nine words.

Between these apparent actions no discrimination is
possible, for an action must be enacted by an actor, and,
since noumenally I am no entity, there is no entity to act. The

functional aspect of noumenality, being devoid of attributes, has no discriminatory faculty that could be applied to phenomenal manifestation. And responsibility is a psychological concept, based upon imagined volitional independence.

Joy and sorrow, pleasure and pain, are affective phenomena, which appear to be experienced by objects, in all degrees of dreaming, as in nightmares and in the "waking" dream of sentient life, whereas the pure functioning of noumenality is devoid of discrimination and is invulnerable.

"The eye sees, but does not look," as Chuang Tzu pointed out more than twenty centuries ago; "you" see, but it is I that am looking. Sentient objects appear to experience and to act, but the functioning thereof is noumenal. There is no actor, ever or anywhere, as the Lotus-Born (Padma Sambhava) revealed, and no deed done, for just as the sought is the seeker of the sought, so that which is done is the doer of the deed—and none such is to be found.

For what I am is the *seeking* which is the sought and the seeker, and the *doing* which is the doer and that which is done.

57 ·~ The Golden Key

ANYONE WHO has perceived the purely conceptual existence of either time or space has held in his mind the key of the gateless gate beyond which lies understanding of the nature of manifestation—that is, of the universe in relation to sentient beings.

How many have used this golden key may never be known, but has a more direct path to that understanding yet been discovered?

For its perception all manifestation depends on the

extension of what is to be perceived—in an apparent spatial dimension, and also on the duration of such extension in a dimension of time. Without these two inseparable media, called "space" and "time," no manifestation could arise in perception.

This is to say that the sensorially perceptible universe is entirely subjected to the concept of space-time in order to have objective existence.

But the independent existence of space-time as a thing-in-itself, i.e., as an objective reality, is as inconceivable metaphysically as it is inacceptable in philosophy or in physics.

If space-time is recognised as a piece of psychic apparatus devised in order to render perception possible, it will be regarded as no more than an inference devoid of any but conceptual existence.

Recognition of the purely conceptual existence of space-time automatically requires recognition of the purely conceptual existence of the sensorially perceived universe which is dependent upon it, and as a result of such recognition both space-time and universe are seen to belong to the objective voidness which is non-manifestation.

58 ·— *This and That*

That (which is "objectivisable") cannot possibly be free.

This (which is not objectivisable) cannot possibly be bound.

If I am apparently identified with that which is objectivisable, that "me" so-created is bound.

If I remain unidentified with what is objectivisable, or if I am released from such apparent identification, I, eternally free, appear to recover my apparently lost freedom.

For I am *This* which is devoid of objectivity as of identity.

What I am not is *That*, which appears to be identified with what is objectivised.

Yes, indeed, it is as simple as that.

Note: The identification in question is conceptual only.

What-I-am-not—is *not I* only in so far as I am conceived as an entity; otherwise what is objectivisable and what is not (phenomena and noumenon) are identical.

What is here stated can be said by you, whatever "you" may be, but never *of* "you," nor *of* "him," "her," or "them," nor—accurately— of "us" (all of which are objects), for only I can ever truly say it, and every sentient being can say it as "I."

59 ·– *Who?*

AS AN entity I am not cognisable, either as a phenomenon or noumenally, which implies that no personal entity can be found either as "me" or as "I."

If no such being as "a me" exists cognitionally, no such being as "an I" exists cognitionally either, for, if the object is not—there is no subject.

The statement "I am, but there is no me" is no more than a pointing finger, for there can neither be a me-object nor an I-subject, because, if either were, both would then be objects.

I neither am nor am not: that is all that can be stated about me. Or, I am the absence of what I am not as well as of what I am, of not being I as of being I.

Absolute absence of I-ness is all that I am conceptually. But absence and presence, being interdependent counterparts in divided mind, noumenally all that I am is the absence of both presence and absence, which is the absence of my absence as I.

This is beyond conception; that is to say that in no manner can it either be conceived or expressed.

But it can be apprehended non-cognitionally, realised non-conceptually, not in thought which is knowledge, but in non-thought or absolute thought which is not thinking but pre-thinking—or spontaneous awareness that is unaware of awareness.

Note 1: In all forms of *advaita*—Vedanta, Ch'an, Zen, Vajrayana, etc. the ultimate question, whether as practice *(hua-t'ou, ko-an, sadhana,* etc.) or as non-practice (the practice of non-practice) is "Who am I?," no matter what sentient being asks it nor how it is asked.

There could never be an answer other than a repetition of the word "Who?"—but that can supply the no-answer which is awakening to understanding of why no answer could be.

Note 2: Someone unused to metaphysical thinking might seek to maintain that a phenomenal (that is apparent) "me" is cognisable, but such a proposition is too superficial for detailed consideration here. Even psychologically there are at least two widely different supposed "selves" in each of us, immediately discernible by duplicating a photograph of each half of a human face (to make a whole face of each half). But these possess no more "ens" (have no more inherent self-nature) than the diverse and innumerable psychic impulses which are expressed in different and often contradictory fashion under the vocable "I," in the course of every day of our lives. The term "me," as applied by a sentient being to his physical appearance, is a colloquial convention and has no bearing on the subject of this proposition.

60 ·— Presence and Absence

As LONG as there is thinking as if by an objective appearance—there is a "you," and "it" thinks that it is bound.

As soon as such a thinking-process ceases there is no "you" to think that *it* is bound.

For no "you" is present when mind is "fasting."

In a fasting mind no I-concept arises. And there is no inferential entity to assume that it is unfree.

There is nothing consistent or permanent in an I-notion. It is recurrent, but no matter how regular the recurrence may appear to be, nevertheless its intermittence is regular also, and its absences are as inevitable as its presences.

These absences are intemporal, which phenomenally appear as a form of permanence, whereas the presences are entirely in temporality.

Presence in duration comports absence intemporally, but temporal absence, being absence of presence, is also intemporal absence. That is why absence of identification with an I-concept comports its intemporal absence also, for it is the absence of a presence in time, and it is eternal in the full sense of outside the sphere of a space-time continuum.

Noumenally, therefore, its absence is permanent.

The reason why nobody is able to believe that he does not exist is—as has been stated—that there is no entity to believe that it does not exist. Less accurately expressed: if there were an entity that maintained that it did not exist, that entity, in maintaining that it did not exist, would thereby demonstrate its existence.

Therefore non-existence, other than as an abstract and inapplicable concept, could not be maintained of itself by any entity. Phenomenally it cannot be said, for it is self-contradictory, since the saying of it, itself refutes it.

Nor can non-entity say that "it" does not exist, for "it" has no entity not to exist. Non-entity can have no entity to say anything. Non-entity cannot even know that "it" does not exist.

Only absence of entity and of non-entity, of the concept of either, could either exist or not exist without consciousness of existence, but such total absence of non-entity as of entity cannot either exist or not exist.

But this apparent presence of a supposed entity can only be such on account of its noumenal absence. If it were not absent in non-manifestation it could not be present in manifestation—which is appearance; that is, if it were not absent noumenally it could not be present phenomenally. Denying the appearance as such, calling it false, illusory, non-existent, is just playing with words: *it is* a psychic phenomenon, neither more nor less, but like any other appearance, it is conceptual, intangible, dream-stuff, entirely devoid of any nature of its own.

All it is—is its noumenal-absence, and only in our noumenal absence are what-we-are neither entities nor non-entities, which is total voidness of "ens."

If a phenomenal "you" is present—its noumenal absence is present also, and the absence of both presence and absence is all that you are.

Note: Phenomenal presence is noumenal absence, the presence being the manifestation of the unmanifested. The negative absence and the positive presence are inseparable; this is to say that the negative absence is noumenally presence whenever the positive presence is noumenal absence.

In this example, whenever an I-concept is phenomenally present ("the false mind arises" in Buddhist jargon) it is also noumenally absent—that is to say that its absence is noumenally present.

Noumenally it can only be present as (its) phenomenal absence or absent as (its) phenomenal presence: phenomenally it is present as its noumenal absence, and when it is absent phenomenally the presence of its absence is noumenal.

61 ·- Self and Other

AN I-CONCEPT is also an Other-concept.

They are inseparable, for the one requires the other, and the other cannot exist without the one.

All Buddhists theoretically accept the "unreality" of an I-concept, though rarely, I fear, in practice or in teaching. We have just considered the reason underlying the power of this concept, and perhaps we have understood why it cannot disappear as long as there is a "we" that continues to think as from a phenomenal object.

But Buddhists in general still more rarely appear to reject an Other-concept, either in word or in deed. Nevertheless the two concepts are inseparable and what applies to the one applies also to the other.

If Buddhism is to take root in the West should we not emphasise the absurdity of the concept of Other, for that is surely a direct means of emphasising the absurdity of the concept of I, each refutation directly contradicting our conditioned misunderstanding?

Moreover as long as there remains the notion of Other, no one can ever be rid of the notion of I, and as long as the notion of I is the centre from which he thinks no sentient being can ever be awakened to the enlightened state which is his.

Note: Have you noticed how misleading that last sentence may be? It appears to imply that there could be an "I," to have a "centre," a "sentient being" to be "awakened," and an enlightened "state" that could belong to him. When mind fasts, no such notions, expressed as from a phenomenal entity, could arise. Phenomenally they may serve a purpose, but noumenally they are *not at all*.

62 ·- An I-Concept, Analytically

THE VOCABLE "I" becomes attached to each impulse that arises in a psychic complex, no matter how mutually contradictory such impulses may appear to be. From this process springs the idea of a multitude of "me"s.

The impulses in question are affective, so that the inferential "I" is affective rather than intellectual.

What is the origin of the vocable "I"? Every "living" phenomenon, every sentient complex must necessarily have a centre, call it "heart" as in China (which is physiologically sound) or "head" as in Europe.

Such centre in itself is as phenomenal as the appearance of which it forms the "heart" or "centre," but its necessary function is the organisation and care of the phenomenon which it controls. Emotions such as fear, greed, love-hate arise on behalf of the phenomenon for which they constitute protection and stimulate survival and perpetuation in the space-time context of manifestation. Consequently the vocable "I," representing this "centre," represents the physical body, and this representation is responsible for the identification which constitutes bondage.

This "centre," then, is the phenomenal basis of an I-concept or ego or self, which is inferential and has no existence in the sense of being capable of independent action as a thing-in-itself. On account of the emotions of physical origin for which this I-concept assumes responsibility, the whole complex has the appearance of an independent entity which it is not—since it is totally "lived" or "dreamed" by the noumenality which is all that it is.

It is this "centre," and every impulse that arises in a psyche, to which is attached the vocable "I," and this it is to which is attributed responsibility for each thought that arises in consciousness and every action of the apparent "individual." It is this, of course, to which the term "ego" is applied, whose functioning is known as "volition." In fact, however, it merely performs its own function in perfect ignorance of what is assigned to its agency.

It was never I and never could it be I, for never could any "thing," any object of consciousness, be I. As has been explained, there cannot be an objective "I" for, so-being, it would have become an object to itself and could no longer be I. That is why "Is-ness" must be the absence of both object and subject, whose integration in mutual absence is devoid of objective existence.

I could never be anything, *I cannot even be "I"*—for all being is determined. Nor could I ever be *identified* with anything objective, and "an I" is a contradiction-in-terms. I am no "thing" whatever—not even is-ness.

63 ·~ Causality or Indeterminacy?

"INDETERMINACY" FULFILLS the same purpose as "Causality." Each is a schematic conceptual structure devised in order to explain the mechanism whereby the universe manifests in its accompanying framework of Space-time.

Statistical probability or inexorable cause-effect? Neither has factual existence other than as an enunciation of a supposed "law" apparently governing an apparent (phenomenal) world evolving by extension in "space" and duration in "time."

In non-manifestation there can be no thing or appearance of a "thing," but total absence of the objectifiable. There can *be* no thing as such anywhere—for no thing has ever *been*, manifested or not; but in manifestation, which *is* objectivisation, "things" are perceived as objects and things appear as such—and constitute the phenomenal universe.

Both manifestation and non-manifestation are conceptual, neither either is or is not except as the absence of non-manifestation.

Therefore a "cause" can only be an integral part of manifestation, dependent on spatial and temporal extension. A "cause" is conceptual, cannot exist as a thing-in-itself, and there is no thing of the kind that could be created or introduced as such into the temporal stream of the manifested universe.

It follows that there is absolutely no action that a sentient being (a phenomenon) can perform in the objective universe as a result of its own volition, for its existence is apparent (phenomenal) only, and there is no entity to act. A phenomenon must be entirely determined by Causality or by Statistical Probability, and there is no entity to be either bound or free.

The notion of an entity, resulting from a subjective identification with a phenomenal object, can only produce a psychic condition suggesting the bondage of such illusory entity to a conceptual causation.

Only events, therefore, can be subject to determination by inferential causation—never a sentient being as *what he is*, the *appearance* of whom is entirely unfree.

Noumenality, which in-forms the phenomenon, is not in

question, for there is no thing (object) there to experience or to suffer in any circumstance. If the phenomenon seems to suffer—that is an affective reaction resulting from his identification; such suffering is phenomenal, and noumenality remains untouched and untouchable.

Only events, which are effects of causes, can become causes, and neither cause nor effect can touch us or reach this-which-we-are.

Thus, as usual, there is no question, for the premises were false.

Never can *we* be determined by causation, but each sentient being may declare: "Causation—that is what I am."

N.B. There is no "we" otherwise than as a colloquial convenience.

64 ⸱⁓ *Aria*

Moderato

THERE IS only I, unconditioned, devoid of attribute or identity.

A mere thought of "me" is instantaneous bondage.

Bondage has no duration apart from the persistence of the concept of "me"; i.e., its apparent duration is coincident with such a concept.

There is no "me," there never has been, never will be, never could be any such entity.

There is no "you," there never has been, never will be, never could be any such entity.

There is no need to read books, chant Sutras, recite Scriptures, perform any antics; there is nothing whatever to discuss, argue about, or explain.

There is nothing whatever to teach or to be learned.

Every living (sentient) being knows this and is free to become aware of it and to "live" it.

All else but this is called "bondage"—and that is an illusory thought conceptually inhibiting pure (non-dualist) vision.

Forte

Every volitional act of reading, chanting, listening, discussing, arguing, explaining, etc. must necessarily reinforce the thought which constitutes "bondage."

No volitional action whatsoever is possible that could "liberate" from "bondage," since there is no entity to be bound or to be free.

All that is possible is awareness of this which is already known, and consciously living this which is already being lived.

All else is appearance, which is phenomenal dreaming.

Fortissimo

To hell, ten thousand hells, with all phantasies based on the notions of "self" and "other"—self judging other, shadow-boxing in false mind, "I" and "you" (I speaking as an object).

I alone can speak, but what is said by me-as-an-object I do not say.

I alone can look, but what is seen by me-as-an-object I do not see.

I do everything, but what is done by "a me" I do not do.

I am neither entity nor non-entity, but the absence of non-entity, the source of all doing, but not the performer of any act. I am the source of all thoughts, but not the thinker of any.

Once more: I am, there is no I but I—but there is no me at all, no you, no him, her, it, no us or them.

And every living being is no being, because all a being is— is I. And I am not.

What here is said every sentient being may say—for every sentient being is I.

And there is nothing else to be said, nothing what ever— and this is already too much.

65 ·— Pseudo-Problems

I

THE QUESTION whether "X" is bound or free—in jargon, "ignorant" or "enlightened"—and the question whether "X" is determined or indetermined—in jargon, "predestined" or has "free-will"—are identical.

Neither is a question at all. Their premises being false, neither question could arise.

There is no "X," no entity, to which either condition could be applied—either physically or metaphysically, either in daily life or in mind.

A psyche-soma is incapable of exercising freedom of any description. It is an appearance that is subject either to a system of apparent causality or to a system of manifestation dependent on statistical probability, which are two manners of envisaging the mechanism of phenomenality.

The noumenal aspect of the phenomenon "X" is inseparable from that of any other phenomenon, being noumenality itself, which, having no objective existence other than its phenomenal manifestations, can have no "ens" which could be subject to any conceptual condition.

If this is used as a standard of reference for all supposed "problems" to which any supposed entity appears to be subject—and nearly all problems will be found to be such—it will immediately be perceived that "problems" as such cannot exist.

II. *Again*

What thinks it is in bondage or is "determined" is what thinks it is a psyche-soma subject to causality or indeterminacy—which is another mode of causality.

Phenomenally a psyche-soma can never be free, for there is no "ens" therein to have freedom, nor any such thing as phenomenal freedom to be had.

But what thinks it is in bondage or free, determined or exercising free-will, is identified in thought with a phenomenal object and *appears* to be subjected to whichever condition such thought is attached.

Consequently "he" who thinks he is free (has free-will or is "enlightened") is as much in "bondage" as "he" who thinks he is bound (is "determined" or "ignorant").

The supposed "problem" does not lie in the presence or absence of the objective conditions of bondage or no bondage, determinacy or no determinacy, but in the presence or absence of the subject of these or of any conditions whatever. And the supposed subject is a concept of identity which appears to be present but which noumenally is absent.

To this which every sentient phenomenon is, whose sole cognisable "being" is all phenomenal manifestation, no such concepts as bondage or freedom, or any concepts whatever, could apply.

66 ·– The Quest

SOMETHING LIKE 99.9% of those interested seem to assume that it is the business of an identity to persuade himself that in fact he is no-entity.

The remaining 0.1% seem to assume that it is the business of non-entity to persuade them that such is all that they as identities factually are.

But all are thereby tacitly assuming that *there is* non-entity, which is then the entity which they believe themselves to be.

Phenomenally there cannot be non-entity without entity, nor entity without non-entity, and noumenally there cannot be either—since both are merely conceptual objects.

What these 100% are seeking, however, is the absence of non-entity (of both positive and negative aspects of entity), but as long as they are seeking there will be an entity (or a non-entity) seeking, and they will never find the *absence* of what is *present*.

That is the whole, the only, "problem"—and it is apparent only. It is apparent precisely because they who are seeking are still identities, and identities cannot find their own absence.

A self-anchored phenomenon cannot find the noumenon which it is, any more than a shadow can find its substance. That is why all practice must necessarily be futile, and why the exercise of volition must necessarily defeat its own ends.

It is vain for an object to seek the subject which it is—for only the subject could seek, and it cannot find itself by seeking—for the sought is necessarily elsewhere than that which seeks it, is in a different moment of time and in a different area of space from those of that which is seeking.

The apparent seeker, however, is what time is and what space is, that is, inferential concepts, and the sought is just another. Seeking and finding are others again.

In the total absence of all such concepts there is nothing to seek, nothing to find, and no entity to do either.

In the abandonment of the quest, of all questing, the questor disappears—and where there is no thing to be found, and no one to seek, "isness" is.

That is why the only possible practice is total absence of practice, the absence of non-practice, since in total absence of practice there is no practiser—and identity is no more.

67 ·- Un-lost and Un-findable

ALL APPEARANCE (phenomena) is produced by psycho-somatic apparatus, and is dependent on such apparatus for apparent extension and for apparent duration.

Psycho-somatic apparatus constitutes a mechanism.

Sentient beings in appearance are the product of that—like all appearance, but their sentience is not that, and is not the product of that mechanism.

What phenomenally we are as sentience is what produces the psycho-somatic mechanism which produces phenomena.

Therefore what-we-are creates the phenomenal universe—including the phenomenal aspect of what each of us is as appearance.

But—as the Buddha and others have so frequently observed—there is no cognisable entity anywhere in the whole set-up.

And so . . .

68 ·~ *The Ultimate Symbol*

I HAVE NO objective existence otherwise than as what is sensorially perceived, for such sensorial perception is all that the term "objective existence" could imply.

Were there no sensorial perception there could not be, or appear to be, any such thing as objective existence, and the converse must also obtain, that were there no objective existence there could be no such thing as sensorial perception.

Sensorial perception thereby is revealed as the subjective aspect of all physical objectivity.

Similarly there could not be, or appear to be, any such thing as a thought (i.e., any image or concept in consciousness) if there were not a perceptive faculty to perceive it, nor any perceptive faculty if there were not objective images or concepts to be perceived.

Apperceptive faculty thereby is revealed as the subjective aspect of all psychic objectivity.

Apparent objective existence, therefore, whether physical or psychic, and perceptive faculty, whether organic or mental, are the objective-subjective aspects, inseparable interdependent counterparts, of all appearance.

It follows that I have no objective existence, either somatic or psychic, otherwise than as an object of subjective perceptive faculty, whose existence is mutually dependent on objects perceived.

Perceptive faculty, however, as such is itself an objective concept in consciousness, and so is existing only in interdependent relation to the subject of that concept.

That subject-object, and all subsidiary subject-objects, alternating in consciousness as one or the other, spinning like tops, can only find their resolution in the negation of both aspects, which negation is necessarily neither.

Such total negation can never have a name, for a name specifies a thought, and a thought is an object that requires a subject.

But even negation requires a negator, duration and a position in which negation can occur—that is, an "ens," time and space.

Those apparent functions can only be fulfilled by what has been termed "consciousness" herein, the implied background or environment of all psychic or physical events.

But "consciousness" is a technical term, and as such is as purely conceptual and objective as any other, whereas what is here required must necessarily imply total voidness of objective existence.

Only one term could fulfill such a condition, could carry such an implication—and that is the nominative singular pronoun "I."

I, as a symbol, therefore, alone, unqualified and unqualifiable, having no attribute, remain—but only on condition that the symbol shall on no account become an object of thought.

What I am then is totality—all that is and all that is not, beginning with what is imagined as consciousness, duration and extension, on which all events depend for their apparent existence.

But whereas I am all and forever—concurrently I am not and never was.

Note: All perceptive faculty, the source of "sentience," in its subjective or functional aspect (as opposed to its conceptual aspect), as what it is in function as opposed to what it is called, is an expression of ultimate subjectivity without which even appearance could not appear. As such it is *prajna,* and that must represent an aspect of this which we are.

69 ~ *Enlightenment as Disappearance of Nescience*

THE CONCEPT of "enlightenment" applied to an individual is obviously great nonsense, for the term denotes a state with which identity is incompatible. No "I" or "me" could ever be "enlightened."

As has been pointed out, an apparent identity may "awaken" to that condition—which is to say that it awakens from the dream of individual autonomy to the normal state which is indicated by the term "enlightenment," or "liberation"—from the bondage of illusory identity.

The term itself, however, is ill-chosen, since it implies someone to be "enlightened," but since phenomenal life is based on the notion of identity, language inevitably carries that implication.

The idea of "enlightenment" implies that the absence of that is the normal condition, whereas the contrary is the fact. That absence is the *current condition* of phenomena precisely because such eclipse of noumenality is what phenomenality is, so that the dis-appearance of that eclipse is at the same time the disappearance of phenomenality and the revelation of the noumenal norm.

It is from the illusion of autonomy that a pseudoidentity awakens, and it is the condition that then obtains, a state of universality, which has been given the name "enlightenment," for an apparent identity bas become aware of its universality, and has returned to full consciousness of the totality that it is.

70 · Apperceiving

Identity of Opposites

THERE IS no non-manifestation apart from manifestation.

But manifestation itself, and in the totality of its sensorial-ly perceptible aspects, is nothing whatever but what is called "mind" (if that be the term employed), because in itself manifestation is no thing at all. Indeed it is not even "mind."

By that I mean to make it clear that objects as such are not composed of mind-stuff: they are not composed of any-thing—for they are not there, or anywhere.

They are just perceptions integral in their perceiving, which perception and perceiving is the supposed "mind" that they are assumed to be.

Nevertheless there is not "a mind," nor anything to take its place (such as "a consciousness"). Its only existence—conceptual at that—*is in manifestation,* i.e., as the phenomenal objects, physical or psychic, which are apperceived.

Objects are seen as nothing but "mind," and "mind" is seen as nothing but objects. That is to say that "mind" only appar-ently exists in order to render that manifestation perceptible, accompanying it as do the concepts of "time" and "space."

There is no "mind": what the term signifies is apperceiving itself.

"Mind," therefore, *objectively regarded,* is all that appears to be, all that everything appears to be, but in fact it is not at all—for there could not be anything apart from the phenom-enon of perception—in the form of apperceiving—and *that* is totally devoid of objective quality and could never in any manner be described, since in any and every such attempt apperceiving must necessarily be the described, that is, the describer, describing what can have no objective quality to describe.

Apart from manifestation manifested there is no such thing as non-manifestation. Manifestation is the only non-manifestation. There is no other non-manifestation at all. To conceive it as "the source" of manifestation, that is, as some thing-in-itself, is as misleading as to conceive manifestation as a thing-in-itself.

There is no other apart from self,
No non-being apart from being,
No non-manifestation apart from manifestation,
Not because that is conceptually inevitable,
But because their mutual existence is Apperceiving.

Note 1: This attempt to record the inseeing of all objects as mind-only should clearly reveal the identity of non-manifestation and manifestation, as of non-being and being, others and self, whose equation Hsieh Yung-chia (A.D. 385-433) tells us *(see* Ch. 52) leads to awakening. He was discussing the words of Tao Shêng *(c.* A.D. 360-434), who was the earliest in China to elaborate the doctrine of Ch'an.

Note 2: If you have not apperceived the importance of this feeble record, please listen once more to Huang Po:

"People neglect the reality of the 'illusory' world." *(p.* 106)

"On no account make a distinction between the Absolute and the sentient world." *(p.* 130)

"Whatever Mind is, so also are phenomena—both are equally real (and, of course, unreal) and partake equally of the Dharma-nature. He who receives an intuition of this truth has become a Buddha and attained to the Dharma." *(p. III)*

Of course you must apperceive it for yourself; until you have done so it is only an idea to which your attention is directed. Perhaps now you may believe how vital it is?

Apperceiving is what is called *prajna* in Sanscrit.

71 ·~ In Fine

THE WHOLE Buddhistic and Vedantic system *(Advaita)* depends on the non-existence of identity, as does the very idea of "enlightenment"—which is reintegration in universality.

I doubt if there is anything else to be understood, since every other element of doctrine is dependent on that, so that such understanding is final.

But in itself it is an impossibility as a thing-to-be-done, since it requires the absence of anyone to do it or *to abstain from doing it.*

Here there is neither doing nor abstaining from doing, but only absence of abstaining from doing—which is the Masters' way of saying "total absence *of any identity* to do or to abstain from doing anything whatsoever."

That is the arrow of an enlightened archer, for—however many such arrows may be loosed—each one must split its predecessor in the bull's-eye—which is the eye which itself is the flight of the arrow.

Note: Since identity is a concept of some thing which cannot be as such, that absence pre-exists as an absence, and since it exists as an absence that absence cannot be obtained—for it is already present as an absence. That also is a reason for the unattainability of "enlightenment" given by great Masters. They have also taught that any attempted "doing" turns the supposed "do-er" away from what he is. The reason for that also is now clear.

Identity is said to be "empty," and "emptiness" implies "not-thereness." Like every concept that ever was or ever could be, it neither is nor is-not there, or it is the total absence of is-not-thereness.

For non-existence or absence are concepts also, and they too neither are nor are-not there, and their only being lies in the total absence of nonexistence and of non-absence.

So that the only being of identity lies in the absence of both identity and non-identity, or the total absence of non-identity.

For that is the eternal and only answer to every question that concerns concepts—and what is not a concept?—and the only possible definition of Is-ness.

Colophon

All It Is

WHAT I AM is forever free. There is nothing in what I am to be bound.

Bondage, and the consecutive suffering—which is all suffering—is entirely dependent on the idea of an objective I, that is "a me." But no such contradiction-in-terms has ever existed, exists, or ever could *be*.

Moreover no object could exist as such either, so how could I exist as an object?

An object, all that is objectified, is appearance. That is what constitutes an object—all that an object is or can be, all that the term was invented to describe.

To be an object is just to be perceptible, which is to appear.

To appear to whom? To be perceptible to what?

Only I can perceive. What else could there be to perceive, which *could* perceive? And whatever I perceive must be my object.

My object is an objectivisation of what I am. What else *could* there be for it to be?

Therefore every object is myself. There can be no thing which is not myself. I am no thing but my objects, and my objects are nothing but I.

What is the use of writing, speaking, lecturing about

anything so simple and so obvious?

There is just nothing else whatever to say or to be said! There never was, and there never will be.

Need I add the obvious? Every sentient being can say it.

N.B. Even by wagging his tail.

Part Five

☙

Dialogues between Ego and Alter-Ego

What is non-objective relation?

> Wherever there are others there is a self,
> Wherever there are no others there can be no self,
> Wherever there is no self there are no others,
> Because
> In the absence of self I am all others.

That is non-objective relation.

72 ·~ Dialogues

I. The Pure Land

Is it possible to be rid of the concept of "other" without at the same time being rid of the concept of "I," or to be rid of the concept of "I" without at the same time being rid of the concept of "other"?

It is not possible.

With which should one begin?

With neither. An identified subject cannot rid itself of either concept.

That is news, bad news! I thought that was what is required of us?

As well be required to scoop up the moon by baling its reflection out of a puddle!

What then?

Until an identified subject knows what he is, he cannot be expected to realise what he is not.

Cannot I say also that until he knows what he is not, he cannot realise what he is?

You can. You should. You must.

There seems to be no way out!

That is why we are not all Buddhas. If it seemed to be possible should we not have done it long ago?

But there must be a way out!

There is no "way," and nothing "out." It is here and now.

Then what is it?

What it is—is quite obvious.

Not to me.

If you can't find it by looking—don't look, if you can't find it by thinking—don't think! It is where there is no looking, and no thinking.

Because it cannot either be seen or thought?

Not at all.

Why, then?

Not because it cannot be seen or thought, but because there is no "one" to look or to think!

Then what does one do?

"One" does not do. "One" does not even cease to do.

And so?

It is better for you to tell me. Is what your identified

subject is—anything he can know?

Surely not.

Is what he is—anything he can not-know?

What he is—is not likely to be an object of knowledge.

Can he see, know, or find what he is or what he is not?

I do not think so.

Why is that?

Probably because what he is looking for, trying to know, seeking to find, is what is looking, trying, seeking?

Exactly. That is the answer.

But is it an answer?

It is the only answer. Finding no "thing," he finds that he is what he is, which is also what he is not.

So that what he is not is what he is?

In so far as words can suggest it.

But does that answer my question?

You asked me how to be rid of the interdependent concepts of "other" and "I." They have been mutually abolished.

So that? . . .

No "other," no "I."

And what I am is also what I am not, and what I am not is also what I am! No room for self, no room for other-than-self! Is that not a definition of Nirvana or of the Pure Land?

It is also a definition of the Kingdom of Heaven.

Is there a historical precedent for such an approach?

There are many. For instance when Hui K'o had "his" supposed mind tranquillised by Bodhidharma, by being unable to find it—that was not the result of his having no mind to find, but because there was no "he" to have anything. The mind was not missing: it was he that could not be found.

It was mind that was looking for mind and not finding itself as an object?

And not-finding was finding!

II. Indeterminacy

I am worried about Causation.

You too?

What do you mean?

Nagarjuna and his friends were worried about it also—quite a long time before the birth of Werner Heisenberg, and they had not the Quantum theory of Planck to tip them the wink.

But Buddhism attaches great importance to Causation.

It does, but the Buddha himself discouraged physical and metaphysical theorising, and the great Masters of Ch'an would have none of it.

I understand that the new "law" of Indeterminacy, which replaces Causality, is now generally accepted where the microcosmos is concerned. Must the same "law" apply to the macrocosmos?

I cannot see how or why it should not. Size is as relative as anything else.

Then a great and vital element of Buddhist doctrine goes overboard?

I only know that where the Supreme Vehicle is concerned there are no vital elements of doctrine, and that all conceptuality has been overboard for a thousand years.

You take it calmly.

On board or over, what difference does it make whether phenomenality, the process of manifestation, is explained by a "law" based on the notion of Causality, or by one based on the notion of statistical probability?

Cause-and-effect seem very obvious, anyone can observe them in operation, and they have been accepted as evident for centuries.

Indeterminacy or statistical probability is obvious also, when you become used to the concept, and is perhaps more in concordance with metaphysical understanding than an inexorable causality which gave Nagarjuna and Chandrakirti bad headaches when they found that it did not bear close analysis.

Then you accept Indeterminacy?

Who on Earth do you think I am to accept or refuse the "laws" invented by learned physicists?

Still, the change-over would be far-reaching and, metaphysically, devastating!

How could it matter what "laws" are invented to explain the mechanism of manifestation? All such "laws" are schematic conceptual structures, each fulfills exactly the same purpose, and neither of these either exists or does not exist outside phenomenality.

So it does not really matter?

No form of objectivisation has any nature of its own. Whether someone sees waves or particles, cyclones or poached-eggs at the other end of a microscope, all are objects and, whatever he thinks he is seeing—that is ultimately what is looking, for what else could it be? I think they have reached that conclusion in their own way, for now they know that the "observer" is a "factor" in whatever experiment they undertake.

Ultimately, no doubt, that is so; nevertheless an understanding of the mechanism of phenomenal manifestation is of importance in the practical aspect of metaphysics.

Very well, then. Study the incidence of Indeterminacy and see if you do not come to the conclusion that it accords quite happily with metaphysical understanding.

Of what aspect of such understanding are you thinking?

Let one suffice for the moment—for the subject is vast! If there is no place for volition in Causality, there certainly is no place for volition in Indeterminacy! That will take you a long way—further, perhaps, than you guess as this moment.

Even if that alone is enough, give me something more to support it.

Any one factor suffices! For all are interdependent. However, cause-and-effect, confined to events—since there is no entity to suffer them—seem thereby to be deprived of an essential element, and the numerical—though not the qualitative—majority of Buddhists have succumbed to the temptation to subject their illusory "selves" to Causation, which makes nonsense of their Master's teaching. Indeterminacy, on the other hand, precludes any such compromise.

Since the existence of an entity can hardly be subject to statistical probability!

Quite so: it cuts the ground from under the feet of those who are tempted to maintain belief in such notions. As long as volition—which also assumes an entity—and Causation, which makes a poor showing without one, are eliminated there may not be any very serious trouble in adapting your thought to this new concept. Indeed my guess is that you will find that it fits better than Causation ever did!

But all the teachings based on Causation? Karma and rebirth for example.

Only dogmas are based on Causation, and dogmas had been rejected by the Masters of the Supreme Vehicle before science ever spoke of causality. They, too, have been overboard for a thousand years: no need to fish them up now!

You are ruthless and uncompromising!

Ask yourself whether Bodhidharma, Hui Nêng, or Shên Hui would have been ruthful and compromising, or ever were? Are you not, perhaps, still looking out as from an imaginary phenomenal centre? Nothing that is true can be seen from there! As "I," remember, you are noumenal!

III. As Far as I Am Concerned

How depressing it is to listen to people, who should know better, talking of themselves as though they really existed!

It might be a mistake to despise them—they may just be honest, refusing to pretend!

But I refer to people who should know that nothing objective can exist as such.

Except phenomenally. I am suggesting that, being well aware that they are still firmly identified, they are unwilling to appear hypocritical by pretending that they are not.

But unless they live *their understanding of what they are not, will they ever be rid of the fixation? Is not that the practice of non-practice?*

As long as it is just a game of "let's pretend"—it is practice, not non-practice, and as futile as any other form of practice.

I cannot reconcile myself to their attitude: they let the side down!

Are you not doing that now?

Perhaps I am, but I cannot believe that we should do that.

Let us realise that their attitude is not merely intellectual honesty, but is also factually exact.

How so?

Perhaps they do "really exist."

Come, come!

As long as they think they exist, they do exist—for existence, which can only be apparent, being entirely phenomenal and objective, is conceptual only, and such is their concept.

You mean that they accept their concept as real?

There is no other reality in the cosmos.

They accept themselves as being what they phenomenally appear to be to others, although they are well aware that they are not in fact that at all!

They are that not only to others, but to themselves as well: if it were not so there would be no "others" either.

So we should wait until there are no "others" before affirming that there is no "self"?

No, we can affirm that there is no self, but preferably only in the company of those who already know that such must be the case, and then only when we simultaneously affirm that there are no others either.

Then there would be no "other" to whom such affirmation could be made!

Quite so.

In fact the affirmation is forever superfluous, for there can never be anyone to whom it can be made?

If there is no "self" of whom it can be affirmed, there can be no "other" either to whom it can be affirmed—and there is no "self" to make it anyhow.

The affirmation of no-self is nonsense, then, and is a contra-diction-in-terms?

The self that speaks does not know, and the no-self that knows does not speak!

Because there is neither self nor no-self—and there is nothing to be said?

There cannot be a self, but don't forget that every sentient being is entitled to say "I am."

Is that really so?

Let us admit that the phrase would be less questionable without the "am."

Even so, who is "I"?

There is no such being.

Then who "am" I?

"Who" denotes an object. As such you are an appearance only.

But you said that every sentient being can say "I"?

Yes, indeed. Noumenally he can say "I," and nothing else whatever, for any additional part-of-speech would make him an object, and as that he is not.

So you do exist?

Surely not. No "you" exists. Only I.

But I too can say it?

Of course, of course.

I thought, for a second, that I had understood.

You do understand, but your conditioned objectivising bangs the door as soon as it opens.

Will it open if I knock?

Not if a "you" knocks: only if "I" knock. Not as long as you look outwards as from an imaginary phenomenal centre, trying to do something or other as your "self." But as "I," remember, you are noumenal.

IV. The Monkey's Banana

"There is no difference between the ignorant and the enlightened."—Huang Po

Do you think that the Sage Kuan Yu is enlightened?

If you yourself are—yes.

But I have no such pretension!

Has he?

I do not know that. Why do you ask?

If he has—then he is not.

Why so?

Because then there would be a self to have such a pretension.

But must he not know?

If there is a self to know, then he cannot know *that.*

But he must have a self to be enlightened!

No self has ever been enlightened.

That amounts to saying that no one has ever been enlightened!

Of course not. How on earth could any "one" become "enlightened"? A phenomenon can imagine it is enlightened or anything else, just as a dreamed personage does in the dream in which he is being dreamed. But when the dreamer awakes the dreamed personages just disappear.

But everybody talks about Sages being enlightened.

If that were the only nonsense people talk, how much easier everything would be!

Then even the Buddha was never enlightened?

Not even the Buddha. I think he said it quite often, but few people pay much attention to what he said—however often they read what is attributed to him.

He said he had not attained *anything.*

Quite so; nor has anybody else—any other body, if you prefer.

But surely the attainment *is what he denied, not the*

enlightened state?

That also, but that is secondary; alone it would be express-ing it inadequately—which he is unlikely to have done.

How is it inadequate?

My dear fellow! That interpretation assumes an autonomous individual *self* attaining or not attaining a "state of mind." The doctrine attributed to the Buddha points out that there is neither an autonomous individual "self" nor any "state" or other conceptual condition whatsoever. Have you never read the Diamond Sutra? If it is too verbose, try the Heart Sutra. Both are categorical on the subject, and Buddhist communities chant the latter every day, sometimes twice.

You mean that there is no "self" to become enlightened, that no phenomenon can ever be enlightened?

One would think that you were attributing some novel doctrine to me!

And there is no such "state" as "enlightenment" at all?

How could there be? Surely nothing could be more ele-mentary!

Then what is "enlightenment"?

Have you never seen a child with a toy? Or a dog with a bone? It is a monkey's banana.

159

But it means a lot to Buddhists: it represents their supreme aim.

That is the function of baubles—a focus of interest and attention.

It means more than that to them.

Yes, it is a symbol, a conceptual representation of what they are and will know when they are rid of their imaginary bondage to externalisation.

If you deprived them of that they would be lost.

On the contrary, as long as they have it they can never be found.

Who has ever said that?

Hui Hai, the "Great Pearl" said it, and others before and after him.

It is a hindrance?

The ultimate and absolute hindrance. According to Hui Hai it is the last obstacle.

Then what does it represent?

It represents all that they are when there is no longer any "them" to be anything!

It is just another futile and hindering concept?

More dangerous, perhaps, than most, than any other. If a phenomenon could be "enlightened" then "enlightenment" would be phenomenal, like inebriation or any other psycho-somatic condition. If it is not phenomenal—and anything the word could mean metaphysically certainly is not—then there is no "self" to experience it.

So the whole idea is all my eye!

Children need toys. Adolescents need them less. The mature are not mature if they need them at all.

So that every time one hears apparently grown-up people seriously talking about "enlightenment" one may laugh?

They may have understood that it neither is nor is not—like many another notion, and yet speak of it because it is a social convention to do so. If they do, they themselves may smile. It can even be useful.

How so?

May not seeing that there could never be a "you" to be enlightened be the means of revealing *this* to which such a shining and tantalising symbol eternally points?

It could be a good pointer?

Wrongly understood, it is a disaster: rightly understood it almost says it!

So that is why Huang Po, and so many others, said that there is no difference between the ignorant and the enlightened?

Yet again, again and again, it is *not* the "ignorance" and the "enlightenment," as objective concepts, which are or are not "different," exist or do not exist, or anything else! It is not *that* which is seen but *this* which is looking, which is devoid of difference, of differential seeing.

You mean that Huang Po employed the object in order to point to its source?

They all did! Turning every direct pointing outwards on to objects is turning every direct pointing away from the truth! To-day it is futile—for we have no Masters to nurse us and to beat us up. The message is always clear before it is misrepresented.

Then the way these statements are given us is misleading?

Perhaps that was done on purpose, but ingenuous transla-tors, conditioned to express every concept objectively, account for much. The sense is clear enough, as it was intended to be, for those able to apprehend.

But then it must be known already?

It *is* known already. What is "misleading" to those who are not ready for it may be the means of revelation to those who are.

It was so spoken to the stupid so that the able might under-stand?

Even to-day it is still possible to see why that was regarded as necessary.

But how can one tell?

By asking yourself whether you are not still looking as from a phenomenal centre that has only an imaginary existence. If so, you will be misled; if not—you will understand at once.

V. Custard-Pies

That black fellow with a crooked nose has written me a most insulting letter! What do you think of that?

What do I think? That as his object you must be an unsympathetic character! Too bad: as the object of the lady who wrote to you last week you were, if I remember correctly, an apprentice saint?

Well, as my *object he is an ill-mannered bastard, and she an amiable optimist!*

No doubt. But it is as well to bear in mind the somewhat elementary detail that objects as such have no existence otherwise than as their appearance and interpretation.

Which is to say that they are pure phenomena?

Phenomena are always pure as far as I understand them.

Which means that they are only what is seen?

Precisely. Or otherwise sensorially-perceived, of course.

So that what is perceived is only the perceiver of it?

A reflection at least of the perceiver. What else could there be to be perceived?

So that he is the unsympathetic character, and I am the ill-mannered bastard?

Is not each sentiment the origin of what you respectively perceive as one another?

Are you sure?

Why be sure? Ask yourself how else you could *be*. As one another's objects could you be anything in yourselves?

I suppose not. But ourselves as our own objects?

Somewhat different from ourselves as other people's objects, and usually rather finer chaps.

Do people generally understand that?

Better ask them. My guess would be that "people" in general face up to very little—no matter how simple and obvious it may be.

But what exactly do you mean when you say, or imply, that everything perceived is a "reflection of the perceiver"? Of the self of the perceiver?

Could there be such an entity—other than as a phenomenal reagent apparatus? All perception is presumably a reflection of what appears in what is conveniently referred to as "pure mind," commonly compared to a non-finite mirror which reflects everything, retains nothing, and has no cognisable existence.

Whose notion is that?

To my knowledge, Chuang Tzu described it first; and like that, and the T'ang dynasty Masters, and their successors, used the simile freely. "Mirror-Mind" has proved a helpful appellation.

Does the "Mirror-Mind" perceive "ill-mannered bastards"?

The "Mirror-Mind," or what the term represents, perceives no thing whatever. Perception is phenomenal, and "ill-mannered bastards," or "sanctity" for the matter of that, is a conceptual interpretation on the part of what may be called a psychic complex.

Then what is there really?

Why, no thing, of course! You are making figments and hurling them at one another—like clowns with custard-pies.

What fools you make us out to be!

That, too, is a custard-pie. "Self and other" are the oldest and most ubiquitous pair of clowns—the very archetypes of all clowns and of all clownishness.

Could one say that such is all that they are?

Surely. Anything else would be to take them seriously.

Even in their bloodshed and criminality, fraud, lying and mutual destruction, envy, hatred, malice and all un-charitableness?

Who is it that takes all that seriously?

Nearly all of us do.

Clowning, clowning, clowns taking themselves seriously! Clowns are notoriously tragic characters in private life.

But life is tragic as well as gay.

Dreamed phenomena experience nightmares as well as pleasant dreams.

I am not happy about all this! Are we really nothing but one another's objects—and our own objects too, of course?

As *objects*—what else is there for us to be? I asked you that before: that question is the only answer to yours.

But as the subjects of each object?

That subject is itself in turn an object, and as an object it too has no being.

But there must be an ultimate—let us call it "subjectivity"?

That is according to the logic of dualistic thinking. That "subjectivity," so-named, thereby becomes itself an object—an object of thought. As "non-objectivity" you can go a step nearer to indicating what can only be intuitively apperceived.

But the nearest is "absence of both objectivity and non-objectivity"—which is not any kind of "thing."

And there we stick?

There you stick—as long as you insist on objectivising as a phenomenon, on looking outwards, on being a subject seeking its object. You stick because here no object is; here no object is because "here" no subject is: and the absence of both is . . . ?

Noumenally—their unification?

Two absences do not make one presence. No two makes a "one"—even noumenally.

Then what?

The sought is the seeker that is no thing, absence is the presence of no presence and no absence. What we are, apart from one another's objects, is the absence of all objects, whereby all objects appear to be!

And we are that objective absence which is all that is?

As such we are also every object that appears to be, for all appearance is our appearance, and noumenally all that is phenomenal is us.

I experience a kind of secret joy in listening to that!

Nonsense, you were not merely listening. You experience a kind of secret joy in *saying* that, because in participating in the saying of it you are being it.

How does that happen?

Perhaps momentarily you leave the fictitious phenomenal centre from which you still habitually operate and, as I, you find the noumenal centre which is what the old Masters referred to as your "true nature"?

VI. The Question

That chap looks worried.

Ask him who there could be to have a care-in-the-world?

Or not to have a care-in-the-world?

Of course.

He'd think it a damn silly question.

So it is.

Utterly ridiculous, of course; who could there be? Quaint notion. Make a man laugh, or a girl giggle.

But who laughs, who giggles?

You mean who is the wiseacre who asks the question, or tries to answer it?

Who knows or does not know who there is or who there is not to have or not to have a care-in-the-world?

Not me anyway!

Evidently. But who knows whatever you *do* know?

I.

Of course—that is the answer.

VII. Bodhisattvas and All

Impossible to do anything for the poor woman! I've tried hard to help her, but I cannot.

How on earth do you imagine that one phenomenon could help another?

. . .

You sound flabbergasted! Is it not obvious?

That's just it! But still . . . still . . . what we all try to do, even must *try to do? Bodhisattvas for example.*

Bodhisattvas don't try to do. They have no need. If they did—they couldn't.

You mean that by not trying—one might do more?

In so far as you are a bodhisattva, at least.

But I have no pretension of being a bodhisattva!

Have they?

To judge by the way they are described, one would assume it, but perhaps in reality they did not have any.

It is well to distinguish between the truth enshrined in Sutras, and the transmission of Sutras themselves via people who did not fully understand them. That is one of the reasons, no doubt, why the Master said to a worried monk "Do not be upset by the Sutra: upset the Sutra yourself instead!"

Which implies?

Understand it as the Master speaking it, not as a pupil searching for somebody else's hidden meaning.

But if we don't know the Master's meaning?

We do know it.

How did bodhisattvas help "all sentient beings"?

Did? Is the job finished and done? ·

Well, are there any now?

Why not?

For instance—who?

Anything wrong with the chap I am talking to?

Me?

No, not "you." Even the Buddha "spoke for fifty years and not a word passed his lips."

You mean that I might sometimes be a bodhisattva?

Never.

Why?

Because there is no such "thing," never was and never will be. It is just a name, a symbol, not any kind of object. It implies a *prajnaic* functioning, not a phenomenon.

And such functioning might operate via this *phenomenon?*

Can you see any reason why it should not?

Yes, the density of my ignorance and incompetence.

Even *your* obnubilation is not without *éclaircies!*

Yau might be able to do it, but . . .

Perhaps—if there were such a one, but so far I haven't found a trace of him!

Well, nor have I!

That does not prevent any phenomenon from functioning *prajnaically.* On the contrary.

So it may be possible even for us to transmit prajna?

There is no such thing as *prajna* to transmit. But what we speak of as pure functioning is ours also.

Then we can act sometimes as bodhisattvas?

There aren't any "bodhisattvas," but what we objectify as such can operate via the phenomena that we refer to as "us."

A happy thought! Makes one feel more like something!

Not sufficiently like a frog or a beetle already? Ask a biologist.

Do you mean that they can, too?

Why ever not?

Is there any actual evidence for such a notion?

Evidence! Fancy wanting evidence for the obvious! Must I disturb the sleep of Maharshi's charming cow Lakshmi yet again? She was fully "enlightened"—to use the conventional jargon—according to Maharshi, who seemed to find it quite normal, even unworthy of comment.

So Lakshmi was a bodhisattva!

If that is what you mean by the word.

And we can all help bodhisattvically by not trying to help?

Even, perhaps, sometimes, in spite of trying to help.

Just by . . . just by being?

No, preferably just by *not*-being—for "being" means "to be

determined"—as the Japanese philosopher Nishida pointed out—and all sentient "beings" are determined and so "lived," by environment—publicity, fashion, and general conditioning.

Because "being" implies self-and-others?

It does—and there are neither.

Without "self" one can help "others"?

Without "self" there cannot be "others."

So what?

Pure non-objective relation.

By being others—they are helped?

No, by being others—they are not "others" at all.

Which is help?

Which is Salvation.

VIII. Seeing

What a disagreeable chap that is, as unpleasant as his brother is charming! Don't you think so?

How could I? Each of those judgments is respectively a coconut and a bouquet thrown at an image in your own aspect of mind, entirely your own construction and unrelated to the phenomena to which you attach the images.

Images in mind?

"Self" and "other," the functioning of dualistic discrimination. Precisely the process condemned by all aspects of
advaïta, called in their jargon "false thought," "discriminating," etc., etc., the very mechanism of "bondage" which at all
costs is to be discarded if intrinsic freedom is to be recovered.

In our language—objectivising a purely subjective concept?

Setting up a guy and shying things at it. Making a
coconut-shy of pure mind!

Then what are *those two chaps?*

Without discrimination, without judgment?

Yes.

Do you remember the words of Hui Nêng to Hui Shun—
sometimes called Hui Ming, which awakened him?
"Without thinking of 'good' or 'evil' (or of 'not so good', as
Paul Reps advantageously emended it in his Gateless Gate
version), remember what you were before you were born."
That was true seeing, *advaita*—non-dualist—seeing, seeing
directly without inference or interpretation, and it opened the
gateless gate.

*I have heard that the "mondo" you quote has awakened many
people, but it does not answer my question.*

You have missed the point: Hui Nêng made his persecutor
stop objectivising, stop making conceptual judgments of

things as objects, and turned his attention straight back to the subjective source. He said in effect: "Stop conceptualising, and be what you always were!"

And that was enough?

Perceiving non-inferentially, seeing the phenomenal universe as-it-is, without judgment, is perception of "suchness," of "as-it-is-ness": the subject of such an object is not then itself an object.

Perceiving non-objectively, which is not personal objectivising?

I think that may be said.

Difficult to say!

Never mind the saying, seeing is enough—from the source!

But what does one see?

"One" does not see. There is neither "one" nor "two," neither "self" nor "other," neither "subject" nor "object." Just a seeing of suchness as such.

Just a seeing which is both see-er and seen?

Which is neither see-er nor seen.

Which is? . . .

Pure non-objective relation.

Non-objective relation between what?

The "relation" is between phenomena, between mutually-dreamed objects, but the seeing is noumenal.

But what can mutually-dreamed objects do?

Nothing, their mutuality is also dreamed.

Then . . .

That is why it is true seeing: there is neither subject nor object, self nor other.

You mean because false or inferential seeing is excluded?

"False or inferential seeing" being conceptual interference.

I think I almost understand! Tell me more.

That is enough. Telling—even when it is possible—only hinders essential apprehension.

Because the essential apprehension is in-seeing?

In-seeing is cut off by out-seeing. In the absence of out-seeing it is present.

But what is present?

The source of all seeing. That alone is presence. In-seeing

does not mean looking in one direction instead of in another, "in" instead of "out," from the same centre, as is commonly supposed, but seeing *from* within instead of *from* without, seeing from the source, which is noumenon, not from manifestation, which is phenomenon.

So it really should be not "in-seeing" and "out-seeing" but "inside-seeing" and "outside-seeing"?

Inelegant and still inaccurate, but certainly less misleading! The one is whole-seeing, the other divided-seeing: that is the essential, for a spatial discrimination could not be correct.

This sounds important?

How could it not be? Perceiving is everything, "Seeing, seeing, seeing," as Rumi cried—and he was not referring to the phenomenally-based observation of objects by subjects, but to noumenally-based in-seeing that is devoid of both!

IX. Non-Objective Relation

What do you mean by the expression "non-objective relation"?

No longer seeing "you" as an object.

You being an object seen by a subject?

Yes.

Must not the object reciprocate by also ceasing to see its subject as an object?

"You" are also the subject of the object that ceases to see you as an object.

But can "non-objective relation" be in one direction only, not mutual?

In the case of a Master it is so, but the relation is potential, for one subject only is absent—and so only one object.

Anyhow, how is it done?

It is not done: it happens.

Happens?

Appears to happen: the "relation"—which no longer is such except phenomenally—already exists.

Then how does it appear to happen?

It is what obtains during an absence of the normally prevalent notion of identity.

Subject lapses as such?

Good!

And it takes its object with it?

Excellent!

But then, *what?*

If the phenomenon referred to as "you" also experiences an absence of identity the non-objective relation is total.

They are then one?

No, neither is.

Which is total . . . harmony?

You are in voice this morning!

And if only one phenomenon is momentarily free from identity, what obtains?

I don't think I know.

Then please guess! I find this important.

That is perhaps an understatement: it is noumenal. Presumably the identity that does not respond by absence remains in the presence of wholeness of mind.

Which is unnoticed?

Probably, or recorded as something like dullness.

Although in fact what obtains is luminous?

Not, perhaps, phenomenally.

Does that happen often?

Ask a Master. I doubt if he loses identity often when his

immediate object is unable to respond.

But can anyone but a Master do that?

I have told you—it is not a doing.

Then can it happen to anyone but a Master?

Of course it can! It is a condition that is eternally present.

Then have you experienced it?

Not more often than you have.

Which is never!

Rubbish! You haven't recognised it, that is all!

Now that you mention it . . . I remember having wondered. . . .

Of course, of course.

But I want to do it!

Then you cannot.

So what?

It is present. You will recognise it.

But can it last?

I doubt if it is subject to the notion of time.

But its duration phenomenally could be measured?

Try presenting a stop-watch to a cybernetic electronic calculator, with detailed instructions to use it at the right moment!

Farceur! *Tell me at least if its duration is appreciable.*

Of course it is!

And is it happy?

I don't like the word.

Joyful?

Better, but not quite right.

Radiant?

So you see—you do know!

X. Words That Mean What They Say

Why are so many words used in the wrong manner in meta-physics?

Words are an objectivisation of subject, and if subject perceives dualistically he perceives an object, and his words describe it. Then he is wrong.

No cure for that except perceiving directly! But can what is so perceived be expressed in words?

Expressed—yes; defined—no.

Words are misused to-day in other branches of study! Why is that?

I do not know, but all have developed a jargon, politics most of all.

You mean the fantastic vocabulary of the Communists?

That is, no doubt, the outstanding example.

As when they call every other country "imperialist," whereas the only empire is their own?

Not only Communists; the projection of "self" on to "others" is elementary in psychology. But the vocabulary you speak of is based on vituperation, using words as ammunition, in order to communicate hatred. That, too, is projection.

Does not that defeat its own end?

It stirs up anger among those who use it; the "others" just laugh, as far as I know.

The process has been carried to a fine art!

Misuse of words is no kind of art, still less is it "fine." On the contrary, it is the worst kind of ignorance. Also, as you have just observed, verbal arrows, so charged with poison, do not reach the enemy but boomerang back to the archers.

So that those who use them are poisoned with hatred?

There is no greater poison, but like many poisons it is also a drug, generates artificial anger, and incites the poisoned to fight.

And what is the effect of misuse of words in metaphysics?

The mechanism is identical with what we have just discussed, but the result is intensification of ignorance.

So what is to be done?

Use words correctly yourself—that is what is to be done. And not only in metaphysics.

You have exposed the nonsense of "enlightenment," etc. as commonly used, which causes people to think that a phenomenal object as such can be transformed into something other than what it appears to be, which is turning them in the wrong direction, or keeping them so turned, but you have never explained to me how people can be expected to believe that they do not exist.

But they are not expected to believe—that or anything else.

How so?

Because there is no identity to believe that it is not such!

You mean that if anyone did believe it, he would thereby still be an identity—because it was he who believed it?

183

Evidently.

Then what can he know?

He can apprehend that what he is, is not what he appears to be phenomenally. Apprehending is not dependent on identity, only knowledge is thus limited.

The distinction in terms is somewhat delicate!

Yes, the Chinese used the negative, which is better; but among ourselves we can say it in positive terms, do you not think so?

You mean "not-knowledge"?

It is neither knowledge nor not-knowledge, but the absence of both.

But you don't explain how that can be. I suppose it cannot be explained.

Why ever not?

Are there not things which cannot be explained?

I doubt it. As I said just now, everything can be expressed, but defined—no.

Well, then, things that should not be explained?

I do not believe that there are any. Ultimate understanding could never be transferred verbally, but every element leading to that understanding can be explained, and should be—to those whose cloud of misunderstanding has become thin enough for the light to shine through it.

Thereby making a rift in the cloud?

Quite so.

Then why not tell me how to perceive that I do not exist?

Because there is no one to perceive that he does not exist.

Sorry! I mean why not tell me how to understand that I am not what I appear to be phenomenally?

Is it not obvious? Better for you to tell me.

But I do not know!

Nonsense, of course you do! I will ask *you* in the ingenuous kind of way in which people talk about that. For instance, why do *you* say that *I* am not what I appear to be phenomenally?*

Tell me, first, who do you think you are?

---

* From here the role of the speakers is reversed. The answerer has become the asker, but the *italic* and roman letters belong respectively to the same speakers.

185

Why, me of course!

And what is that?

Me? This here, what I am.

And what makes you think that?
Everybody sees me, and I see myself, part of myself at least, and the whole of me in a looking-glass.

But that is only an object, other people's objects and your own, perceived by senses and interpreted by a psyche on the basis of mnemonic impressions.

What is wrong with my being an object?

Nothing except . . . except that an object is only a notion, an idea, a concept, an image in a psyche.

You mean that is all that I am?

Well, let me see . . . as an object, yes, of course, that is all that you are. An inference.

But I still am as myself!

Well, yes, I suppose you are—in a way.

Why "in a way"? In a big way! And how!

Yes, of course, in a very big way indeed, but not, you see, as a "self."

You mean that the "self" part is only what you call an object?

Quite so. That is all it is. Just a notion, an idea, an image in mind—purely theoretical.

So that what I am is, well—I?

Yes, always I. Like what I am, and everybody else every living thing that can feel "I," which is sentience.

So that in a sense I am everything?

Everything is I—but not then as any kind of object.

Why should that be?

Surely you can see that? Any kind of object is only something perceived: *it is nothing whatever in itself! "I" alone could* be: *all else is* perceived, *and that cannot be anything but I.*

But including what you appear to be as an object?

Yes, that too, of course.

How can that be? What about subject-object?

Subject–object is just object which is nothing but its subject, and subject which is nothing but its object!

So that I am beyond subject-and-object?

Of course, of course! I am pure noumenality! And no thing at all.

So that is what I am when I understand that I am not what I appear to be phenomenally! You have explained it so clearly that I am inclined to think I have understood.

If you are inclined to think that—then you haven't! Such understanding is not possible to an identity!

Good, good! I am not an identity which understands something: understanding that there is no one to understand and nothing to be understood *is* understanding what I am! Fine, and you?

I? Good lord, I had forgotten about myself! And that we had changed places. Is that all it is? But it is quite simple!

And obvious. You knew it, as I told you, but you had not re-cognised it.

XI. Who Was the Buddha?

You people talk a lot about the Buddha, but who was the Buddha?

Does that matter?

It may not, but some people think it does, and I do.

How could I know who the Buddha was?

Does not somebody know?

Many people imagine that they do, but usually it is only a tradition that they have been taught.

Is not that tradition reliable?

No more than any other of the same age and degree.

You mean that it is myth-enshrouded and does not ring true?

Inevitably.

How so?

His words were not committed to writing until some four centuries after his death—and then in another language than that in which he spoke.

So that he cannot have spoken them?

Hardly as recorded.

Which are the more likely to be genuine?

That is for experts to answer. He is credited with so many that had he spoken them all he would surely have died of laryngitis at a comparatively early stage of their elaboration.

Cynic!

Nonsense. They contradict one another. And some can be fairly accurately dated by internal evidence to comparatively late periods during which the doctrines concerned were being developed.

I thought they had all been accurately attributed to different periods of the Buddha's career, in accordance with the kind of people to whom he was speaking?

That is so. Such arrangements represent an immense labour which may satisfy the simple-minded, but which scholars are unable to accept otherwise than with a broad smile.

Then tell me who you think the Buddha was, and what he actually taught.

Why do you ask me such a question? How on earth could I know? I am not only not an expert, but not even a student of the subject.

I know that. Nevertheless you might have some suggestive ideas about it.

Not even that! I can only point out what must surely seem obvious to anybody who knows anything about the matter at all.

And what is that?

What would you expect the Buddha to have been but the last of the six or seven Abbots or Patriarchs of the Nepalese "church" which was in revolt against the Brahmans?

There was such a succession of Abbots and Patriarchs?

I have heard that they are reasonably well recorded and documented in Nepal.

And what was their doctrine?

I think we may conclude that it was epitomised, and brilliantly brought to maturity, by Sakyamuni.

You have just been pointing out that the Sutras teach divers and even contradictory doctrines. May not some of these Sutras have been preached by his predecessors?

Your suggestion, as far as I am aware, has never been made. The proposition that different categories of Sutra represent different aspects of the doctrine, elaborated and preached by different Patriarchs or "Buddhas," all subsequently attributed to Sakyamuni is certainly worthy of consideration. That, however, does not alter the fact that some are of late compilation.

Several independent traditions may have been preserved by communities dating from different Patriarchs, each being subsequently subjected to elaboration before being committed to writing?

I am inclined to agree. Their independent origin might readily have been lost.

Then which should be the oldest?

I can only guess. Surely it would have been the simplest and most comprehensible, largely ethical, teaching now represented by the Pali Scriptures in which, no doubt, it was elaborated considerably during the centuries before it was turned into Sutras. Sakyamuni himself spoke in Maghadi.

So that the Mahayana Sutras are all later inventions?

You speak like a Theravadin! If my opinion is worth anything—which is not my own belief—I see nothing impossible, even improbable, in the Buddha, or another of the Patriarchs, having transmitted an esoteric doctrine to selected disciples, a doctrine or a non-doctrine that was always apart and which eventually re-emerged as Mahayana. But even if it was Sakyamuni, is it not probable that he inherited that also? If he was in fact a member of the family of a Rajah, he was probably "papabili" for the "patriarchate" by birth rather than by vocation. In his case, however, he had the vocation also.

Why have we never heard of this succession of Nepalese Patriarchs or Abbots?

You have, but transformed into a series of prehistoric "Buddhas" stretching over an impossible number of aeons.

You mean that in actual fact they were just a succession of Abbots?

I have been given to understand that they are historically known as such.

Down to Sakyamuni?

As I have said, I have not studied the question at all, but I think down to Maitreya, who may have been the "Buddha" elect, but who never succeeded and, instead, was recorded as the Buddha to come.

Do you really not know what documentary evidence there is for all this?

I really do not. I only know that some exists, and that the historical Sakyamuni's stupa was found, excavated, and the inscription recorded.

Why have I not heard of that?

Have you not? It is quite well known. It may have been sent to Coventry, as such things are apt to be when they upset a myth, though there is nothing scandalous about the inscription except that it applies to a worthy man and not to a deity.

You have kept all this from me!

Not at all. Is it necessary to offend other people's beliefs, even if one were qualified to do so, which I am not?

But historically it is of great interest!

I agree with you. As soon as you asked, I told you the little I know.

I am not sure that it does not increase my admiration for Buddhism, rather than the contrary.

I think it should. The shroud of myth only throws discredit on the teachings—since to-day people cannot be expected to believe the incredible.

The more credible historically it is, the greater the force it should have?

That is my view also.

And this account is very credible, is it not?

Personally I think it is *trop vraisemblable pour ne pas être vrai;* moreover and anyhow—"se non è vero è ben trovato!"

It seems obvious to me already—now that you have pointed it out. Buddhism is the better for it, nor does it contradict, or even upset, the picture the Buddha left of himself in the earlier Sutras!

We have only to leave the old scholars to clear the matter up in their own good time. Few of them like annoying the superstitiously religious.

Like getting into the bad graces of a swarm of bees! Who can blame them? But they cannot prevent us from believing it.

Nothing could induce me to believe it! Or anything else. Belief is futile—for there is no one to believe. I merely suggest that a historical instinct insists that this account of the origin of Buddhism is redolent of truth. Faith is the stupidest thing on earth—and roundly condemned by the Buddha!

All "faith" is stupid?

Surely not. The word means "belief in authority" but what is "authority"?

Perhaps that depends upon whose? On whose does this depend?

Tradition and superstition for the most part. Only knowing is believing, and such believing is being; such "being" is another kind of faith, the kind to cherish.

And the kind in question is the former?

May not anyone judge for himself?

Index

References are to the numbered sections. Certain terms such as noumenon and phenomena, subject and object, self and other, etc. which occur very frequently in the text will not be found in the index. The aim of this index is to enable readers to find a chapter in which they remember some technical term or other feature.

Other Spiritual Classics by Wei Wu Wei

⚮

Fingers Pointing Towards the Moon, Foreword by Ramesh S. Balsekar

The first book by Wei Wu Wei, who wrote it because "it would have helped the pilgrim who compiled it if it had been given to him."

ISBN 978-1-59181-010-0 • $16.95

Why Lazarus Laughed

Wei Wu Wei explicates the essential doctrine shared by the traditions of Zen Buddhism, Advaita, and Tantra, using his iconoclastic humor to drive home his points.

ISBN 978-1-59181-011-7 • $17.95

Ask the Awakened, Foreword by Galen Sharp

Ask the Awakened asserts that there are no Buddhist masters in present western society, and we must rely on the teachings of the ancient masters to understand Buddhism.

ISBN 978-0-9710786-4-2 • $15.95

All Else is Bondage, Foreword by Matt Errey

Thirty-four essays, based on Taoist and Buddhist thought, constitute a guide to what the author calls "non-volitional living"—the ancient understanding that our efforts to grasp our true nature are futile.

ISBN 978-1-59181-023-0 • $13.95

The Tenth Man, Foreword by Dr. Gregory Tucker

In giving us his version of the perennial philosophy, Wei Wu Wei brings a very different perspective to the conventional notions about time, love, thought, language, and reincarnation.

ISBN 978-1-59181-007-0 • $15.95

Posthumous Pieces, Foreword by Wayne Liquorman

This work was not published after the author's death. Rather, these profound essays and epigrams are "tombstones, a record of living intuitions."

ISBN 978-1-59181-015-5 • $15.95

Unworldly Wise

Wei Wu Wei's final book is an enlightened parable in the form of a conversation between a wise owl and a naïve rabbit about God, friendship, loneliness, and religion.

ISBN 978-1-59181-019-3 • $12.95

Sentient Publications, LLC publishes books on cultural creativity, experimental education, transformative spirituality, holistic health, new science, and ecology, approached from an integral viewpoint. Our authors are intensely interested in exploring the nature of life from fresh perspectives, addressing life's great questions, and fostering the full expression of the human potential. Sentient Publications' books arise from the spirit of inquiry and the richness of the inherent dialogue between writer and reader.

We are very interested in hearing from our readers. To direct suggestions or comments to us, or to be added to our mailing list, please contact:

SENTIENT PUBLICATIONS, LLC
1113 Spruce Street
Boulder, CO 80302
303.443.2188
contact@sentientpublications.com
www.sentientpublications.com